☞ **W9-DFU-158**

CULTURES OF THE WORLD

EGYPT

Robert Pateman

MARSHALL CAVENDISH
New York • London • Sydney

Reference edition published 1993 by
Marshall Cavendish Corporation
2415 Jerusalem Avenue
P.O. Box 587, North Bellmore
New York 11710

Editorial Director	Shirley Hew
Managing Editor	Shova Loh
Editors	Tan Kok Eng
	Leonard Lau
	Siow Peng Han
	MaryLee Knowlton
Picture Editor	Yee May Kaung
Production	Edmund Lam
Art Manager	Tuck Loong
Design	Ang Siew Lian
	Ong Su Ping
Illustrators	Lo Chuan Ming
	Kelvin Sim
Cover Picture	Christine Osborne

Printed in Singapore

Originated and designed by
Times Books International
an imprint of Times Editions Pte Ltd
Times Center, 1 New Industrial Road
Singapore 1953
Telex: 37908 EDTIME Fax: 2854871

Library of Congress Cataloging-in-Publication Data
Pateman, Robert, 1954–
        Egypt / Robert Pateman.
            p. cm.—(Cultures of the world)
        Includes bibliographical references and index.
        Summary: Discusses the geography, history, government,
    economy, and culture of the Middle Eastern country that at one
    time had the most advanced civilization the world had yet seen.
        ISBN 1-85435-535-X (vol.) :   —ISBN 1-85435-529-5 (set)
        1. Egypt—Juvenile literature.   [1. Egypt.]   I. Title.
    II. Series.
    DT49.P38 1992
    962—dc20   92–10209
                                                                  CIP
                                                                  AC

INTRODUCTION

FOUR THOUSAND YEARS ago, a mighty civilization grew up along the warm fertile banks of the River Nile. United under the rule of the powerful pharaohs, Egypt developed the most advanced society the world had ever seen.

Great temples and pyramids were constructed and music, medicine, art and the sciences flourished. The disciplined Egyptian armies dominated the region, making Egypt the world's first great "superpower."

Today, Egypt faces many problems as it struggles to provide better care for an ever increasing population. Yet, the Egyptian people can also look back on many recent achievements, and modern Egypt is a proud and independent nation, willing to play a leading role in regional and world affairs.

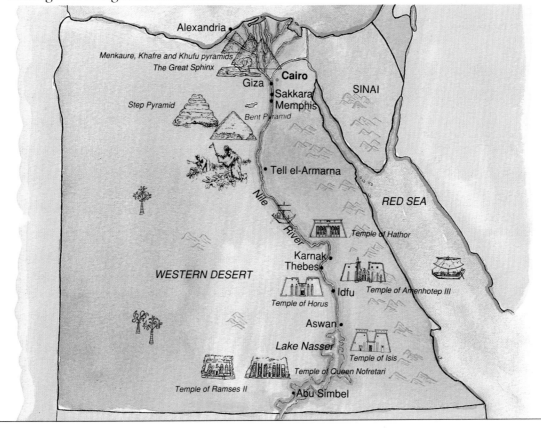

CONTENTS

A nomadic Bedouin and his camel.

CONTENTS

A mosque in Cairo.

GEOGRAPHY

EGYPT is situated in the northeast corner of the African continent. Covering 386,650 square miles, which is about equal in size to Texas and California combined, it is the twelfth largest country in Africa. Egypt is bordered on the west by Libya; on the south by Sudan; on the east by Israel, the Gulf of Aqaba and the Red Sea; and on the north by the Mediterranean Sea.

Egypt receives very little rain and consists largely of desert. However, the Nile River runs through the country, creating a fertile green valley. North of Cairo the river widens out to form the Nile Delta. Ninety percent of Egypt's population crowds into the valley and delta.

West of the Nile is the Western, or Libyan, Desert. There are some fertile oases in this desert. To the east lies the Eastern Desert or Arabian Desert which is more mountainous and barren.

Opposite: **Although much of Egypt's terrain is low-lying desert, rugged mountains can also be found along the Red Sea and in the Sinai Peninsula.**

Left: **The Rosetta channel, on the west Nile Delta. It was silt deposited by this waterway and other tributaries of the Nile that makes the Delta so fertile.**

Egypt may be divided into four main regions: the Nile Valley and Delta, the Western Desert, the Eastern Desert and the Sinai Peninsula.

NILE VALLEY AND DELTA

The Nile is one of the world's greatest rivers. The Greek historian, Herodotus, was quite correct when he described Egypt as being "The gift of the Nile." Starting south of the equator in the heart of Africa, the Nile flows northward out of tropical Africa into desert land, transforming the barren land surrounding it, before emptying into the Mediterranean.

Altogether the Nile is just over 4,000 miles long, and approximately the last 1,000 miles run through Egypt. By taking water from the river, the Egyptians have been able to create a thin green valley of fertile land that runs the length of the country. This flood plain that forms the Nile Valley is usually about six miles wide, but in places it can be much narrower.

When it reaches the Delta, the Nile breaks into hundreds of different branches. This creates a fertile, fan-shaped area that is 100 miles long and 155 miles wide by the time the river finally reaches the sea. There are two main channels through the Delta, the Damietta and Rosetta channels, both named after the major cities along their course. Sixty percent of Egypt's useable land is located in the Delta. Ironically, the Delta has several shallow lakes and swamps which are too salty to be used for cultivation.

In the past, the African rainy season would increase the amount of water flowing into the Nile, and produce the annual floods. The creation of the Aswan High Dam has, however, changed this ancient pattern, and the last flood occurred in the mid-60s.

Two miles long and 364 feet high, the Aswan High Dam took ten years to complete. When it was opened, it created a gigantic artificial lake, Lake Nasser, that stretched back across the border into Sudan. The annual flooding of the Nile is now controlled and land that was once under water for long periods can now be used to produce two or even three crops a year.

THE WESTERN DESERT

Two thirds of Egypt is covered by the Western Desert. This is part of the Great Sahara, that stretches across north Africa all the way from the Atlantic coast to the Nile Valley. There are a few mountains in this desert, with Gebel Uwainat in the far southwest being the highest point at 7,000 feet.

More impressive than the mountains are the great depressions that can drop several hundred feet below sea level. The largest is the Qattara Depression which covers 7,000 square miles. Qattara starts just south of the Mediterranean coast and at 436 feet below sea level is the lowest point on the African continent. There are ambitious plans to build a canal to the Mediterranean Sea and so turn the Depression into a great lake. Such a large area of surface water might change the whole desert environment.

For the most part, the Western Desert is a flat sandy plateau. Close to the border is an area known as the "Great Sea of Sand." Here you will find the type of sand dunes that form most people's idea of a true desert. The shape and movement of the sand dunes is controlled by the wind. Some dunes may move a few hundred feet a year, while others are almost stationary.

The Western Desert is composed of great ridges of blown sand. It is not unknown for sand dunes to be 600 feet high and 100 miles long. If they come near cultivated areas, they can cover roads, or swallow up whole villages.

9

Few spots in the world are as inhospitable as the heart of this great desert, where temperatures can rise as high as 120 F. However, at night, there is no cloud cover to retain heat, so the temperature might drop to freezing. In addition to the lack of water and high temperature, the desert is subject to strong winds that blow constantly from the northeast. In 524 B.C., a 50,000-strong Persian army disappeared while trying to march across the desert to Siwa.

However, the desert is not totally barren, and except where there are shifting sand dunes, some forms of life will survive. The desert has its own species of birds, snakes, scorpions and lizards.

With a population of over a million people, Al Fayyum is the largest oasis in Egypt. Waterwheels abound in Al Fayyum, where abundant water has turned it into a wonderful fertile garden.

There are six major oases in the Western Desert. These isolated fertile "islands" grew up around spring water, and are usually found in depressions. Palms trees and other crops will grow here, supporting a human population. Today, top quality dates are packed in factories within the oases and sent by truck to Cairo.

THE EASTERN DESERT

The Eastern Desert, which is also known as the Arabian Desert, starts at the Nile and runs east to the coast. A mountain range borders the Red Sea. Long ago this was a fertile area, and it still has ancient valleys called "wadis" that were once riverbeds. There are also impressive fossilized forests where the sand is littered with millions of ancient trees, now turned to stone.

It was once thought that human habitation was limited to the coast, but two tribes have recently been discovered living a nomadic life in the Arabian Desert. Recently the coast has become an important center for the Egyptian oil industry. The coastal town of Hurghada is even being developed for tourism.

THE SINAI PENINSULA

The Sinai is a barren desert peninsula. Geographically, it is really more part of Asia than Africa. It is bordered by three seas, the Gulf of Aqaba to the east, the Gulf of Suez to the west and the Mediterranean to the north. Since the building of the Suez Canal, the Sinai has been physically cut off from the rest of Egypt.

In ancient times, the Sinai was a wild and inhospitable desert area that formed a formidable barrier between Egypt and her Middle Eastern neighbors. The ancient Egyptians did little in the region except send the occasional mining expedition in search of turquoise or other minerals.

In the north, the Sinai is a flat and sandy desert area. The south is far more mountainous and Gebel Katherina is the highest point in Egypt at 8,652 feet. Gebel Musa, the traditional Mount Sinai, is another impressive peak and rises to 7,497 feet.

The Bedouin people have always lived in the Sinai, traditionally as nomads, moving from oasis to oasis. In ancient times they were fierce warriors and the Egyptians only entered this area under military protection. Today, many of them have abandoned the nomadic way of life, and instead make their living from a combination of date farming and raising livestock.

Serrated mountain ridges are a striking feature of southern Sinai. Egypt's highest peak, Gebel Katherina, is located here.

THE SUEZ CANAL

The Suez Canal is a man-made waterway that links the Mediterranean with the Red Sea. It is 118 miles long and 64 feet deep—big enough to allow ships of up to 150,000 tons to pass through.

The first stretch of the canal runs from Port Said ("sah-EED") on the Mediterranean, to the city of Ismailiya, which is on the shores of Lake Timsah. A smaller section of the canal links this lake with the Bitter Lakes. From here a third section continues to Suez and the Red Sea. Three convoys a day make the 15-hour trip through the canal, and the route cuts 6,000 miles off the journey between Europe and Asia.

The canal was inspired by a Frenchman, Ferdinand de Lesseps. In 1854, he obtained permission to commence the project from the Egyptian Khedive, and the following year an International Technical Commission examined the possible routes. By 1858, the Suez Canal Company had raised around $40 million in stocks. Work commenced in 1859 and was to last for ten years.

On November 17, 1869, a fleet of ships assembled in Port Said harbor to make its maiden sailing through the canal. They arrived in Suez three days later, having been entertained en route at a ball given by the Khedive. Since then the Suez Canal has become the busiest stretch of waterway in the world and it has been enlarged several times to meet the needs of a new generation of ships. The canal was closed between 1967 and 1975 as the result of the Arab-Israeli war.

CLIMATE

Egypt is a hot and dry country. However, there can be a marked difference between winter and summer temperatures. In Cairo, temperatures can rise as high as 95 F in summer, and drop to as low as 45 F in winter. Farther south, the country becomes hotter. Winters in Aswan are pleasantly warm, but summer temperatures can reach 107 F.

Alexandria, in the north, enjoys much milder weather than the rest of the country. Here, the highest temperature throughout the year will not usually be more than the mid-80s, and the cool breezes of the Mediterranean make even the hottest days pleasant.

Egypt gets hardly any rain or clouds. Cairo will average about five

Top and bottom: **Dates are Egypt's commonest fruit, and at least 30 varieties of date palms are grown in Egypt.**

rainy days a year, and sometimes less. Most of this rain will fall between November and January. Siwa, an oasis in the middle of the great Western Desert, might only get rain once or twice every century. Therefore, away from the influence of the Nile, Egypt quickly becomes a desert land.

FLORA AND FAUNA

Of Egypt's natural plant life, papyrus ("pah-PIE-rus") is one of the most interesting and useful. It is a water reed which was used for making paper in ancient times. Today, it can no longer be found in the wild, and only grows where cultivated. The date palm is the most common native tree, found throughout the Delta, in the Nile Valley and in the oases. The acacia is widely distributed, as are eucalyptus and sycamore. In the desert areas, coarse alfa grass, stunted tamarisks as well as a great variety of thorny shrubs and herbs can be found.

Egypt is a desert land, without any forest. Because of this lack of tree cover, Egypt has relatively few large animals. The camel is the creature most people associate with Egypt, but these "ships of the desert" were introduced to the country as a domestic animal. There was more wildlife along the Nile in ancient times, and tomb paintings show ostriches, crocodiles, hippopotamuses and even giraffes. Pressure from the human population has eliminated these animals, although there are occasional, but unconfirmed, reports of ostriches being seen in remote areas.

Magnificently adapted to life in the harsh desert, where there is often little food or water, the camel is still widely used as a means of transportation in Egypt today. Camels can drink 100 quarts of water in one go, and then go for days without drinking.

Today, a few larger animals still survive in the desert. These include the gazelle, the hyena and the jackal. There are also small numbers of wild boars, lynxs and wild cats that survive in the Delta region.

Egypt has thirty-three species of snakes, half of which are venomous. Some of the more spectacular species include the Egyptian cobra, the horned viper and the hooded snake. Of these, the Egyptian cobra has a reputation for being particularly aggressive. There is a good variety of lizards, scorpions and insects, but very few butterflies.

Egypt has particularly impressive bird life. There are approximately 200 species which migrate, and 150 resident species. The Nile Valley is a very important flight path for birds migrating between eastern Europe and East Africa. The fertile valley provides food for these migrating birds, which also use the river for visual navigation.

Some of the world's most beautiful birds, such as the golden eagle and lammergeier, can be found in the Eastern Desert and the Sinai. Although no storks and few ducks breed in Egypt, many of these species use the lakes as feeding grounds. One of the most common birds in Egypt is the hoopoe, a small but colorful ground feeder with a crest-like fan.

Egypt's most colorful wildlife can be found under water, in the coral gardens of the Red Sea. The coral gardens are home to a vast variety of fish, including potentially aggressive animals such as tiger sharks and moray eels. Over 190 varieties of fish, including large perch, carp and burl, live in the Nile.

CAIRO

Cairo sits strategically between the Nile Valley and the Delta, about a hundred miles from the coast. One out of every four Egyptians lives in the capital, the political and commercial center of the whole country.

Cairo's population is about 13 million, making it one of the ten largest cities in the world. The population is increasing at a frightening rate, largely due to people moving in from the countryside to seek work. This has created terrible problems, and the city once described as "mother of the world" now often looks more like a tired and worn-out grandmother!

The Nile cuts through the city and there are two large islands, Roda and Zamalek. Tahrir Square is generally considered the main center of the city. Traveling east from Tahrir Square you pass Opera Square, the Presidential Palace, and beyond that the old city with its wonderful mosques and city gates. The west side of the Nile has fewer tourist sites, but is home to the University of Cairo and the middle class neighborhoods of Muhandisin and Doqqi. From here, four lane highways run out to the pyramids which now mark the edge of the city. The modern center of Cairo is relatively small, and apart from one or two wealthy suburbs it is really a great collection of villages that have found themselves caught up in the middle of a vast city.

Cairo is the capital city of Egypt and is home to nearly 25% of the population. The capital is an interesting blend of old and new. Here, historical monuments, such as the pyramids of the Egyptian pharaohs and ancient mosques and Coptic churches co-exist with modern buildings and offices.

ALEXANDRIA

Alexandria is Egypt's second largest city with a population of just under three million people. It is situated on the north Mediterranean coast and is a major international harbor. As the name suggests, it was founded by Alexander the Great, and in Greek times was an important center of commerce and learning. The Alexander Lighthouse, which once stood here, was considered by some to be one of the Seven Wonders of the Ancient World, while the world's first great public library was founded here.

Today, Alexandria enjoys a more cosmopolitan atmosphere than the rest of Egypt. The cooling Mediterranean breezes give it a pleasant climate, and many summer homes are built close to the beaches. The city has a good museum and a well-preserved Roman amphitheater. In addition to the usual forms of transport, central Alexandria is linked by a tram system. On the outskirts, Alexandria has a large industrial area which has been located here to take advantage of the harbor facilities.

EGYPT'S OTHER CITIES

ASYUT is an important commercial center and university town in central Egypt with a large Coptic population. In the past, it was a major resting point on the caravan route. Today, it is a center for cotton spinning and pottery.

ASWAN Situated deep in southern Egypt, Aswan is the last major town before the Sudanese border. In ancient times, the pharaohs quarried some of their best granite from this area. Today, it is famous for the High Dam, and several industries, including a fertilizer plant, have been located here.

A fleet of feluccas on the Nile at Aswan paints a picturesque scene. For thousands of years, feluccas have plied the Nile River, using it as a major transportation artery.

LUXOR is a resort town in Upper Egypt whose wealth is based around its ancient treasures. It stands on the site of ancient Thebes, which was the capital of Egypt for much of the pharaonic period. Luxor is linked to Cairo by good rail and road connections, and has an international airport.

PORT SAID was founded in 1856 on a mud and sand strip between a lake and the Mediterranean Sea. Since then it has grown into a city of nearly half a million people. It is Egypt's second largest port, and a free trade zone where many Egyptians go to buy foreign electrical goods.

SUEZ Suez, and Port Tawfiq, guard the southern end of the canal. The ancient Egyptians built a fortress in this spot, and the present city was founded in the 15th century. Although Suez was almost totally destroyed in the 1973 war, the reopening of the canal and the oil boom has seen it prosper. Today, it is a thriving city of nearly half a million people.

17

HISTORY

EGYPT WAS THE HOME of one of the world's first great civilizations. An advanced culture developed around 4,000 years ago, and lasted for over 2,000 years. It is worth remembering that Christopher Columbus discovered America in 1492, so that modern American history, in contrast, is still only 500 years old.

This ancient Egyptian civilization developed the world's first national government. Their inventions include a paper-like material called papyrus, a form of writing that used pictures, and a 365-day calendar. They were also noted mathematicians, poets, doctors and soldiers.

Most of all, however, the ancient Egyptians are remembered for their building achievements, and many of their magnificent temples and pyramids still survive today.

THE START OF EGYPTIAN HISTORY

Around 5,000 years ago, small villages and communities started to develop along the Nile Valley. The soil here was wonderfully fertile and people abandoned the old hunting way of life to become farmers. At the same time the desert protected them from invaders, and the area prospered. The population grew and the villages grouped together until they formed two strong kingdoms.

The Kingdom of Upper Egypt was established in the Nile Valley, and the Kingdom of Lower Egypt was centered in the Delta.

About 3100 B.C., a powerful king of Lower Egypt united the two kingdoms and founded the first dynasty. He established his capital at Memphis, which is very close to the site of modern-day Cairo. We are not really sure how he achieved this, but a stone palette in the Cairo Museum shows the king ruthlessly slaying his enemies. In legend, this king was called Menes ("MEH-nez"), although his real name was more probably Narmer.

Above: **Papyrus art. Papyrus was used for thousands of years by the Egyptians for making paper.**

Opposite: **A man contemplates the immenseness of a necropolis' temple. In ancient Egypt, necropolises such as this were located just outside the city proper, mainly on the edge of the desert. Called "city of the dead," a necropolis is a large and important burial area, where pyramids, temples and tombs were built and maintained for those who could afford an affluent afterlife.**

Measuring 413 by 344 feet at the base, and standing 200 feet high, the Step Pyramid of Sakkara was the oldest stone structure of its size in the world. Like the later pyramids, the Step Pyramid complex was both a royal tomb and a temple.

THE OLD KINGDOM

By the start of the third dynasty, around 2686 B.C., Egypt was firmly established as a nation under a strong central government. It was this third dynasty that was to build the greatest monuments the world had ever seen —the pyramids of Egypt.

The first of the pyramids was built to house the body of King Zoser. It started off as just a large tomb, but was redesigned several times to create a towering pyramid that climbed nearly 200 feet, in six giant steps. This Step Pyramid was the masterpiece of Imhotep, chief advisor to the King, and one of the most remarkable men of the age. Apart from being an architect, Imhotep was a priest, scientist, doctor and writer. His achievements were so remarkable that later generations worshiped him as a god.

Each pharaoh now tried to outdo his predecessors with the size and grandeur of his pyramid. Snefou, one of the great kings of this period, actually built two pyramids. The first is known as the Bent Pyramid because of its unusual shape. Snefou's second tomb was the first true pyramid. It is

called the Red Pyramid because of the pink limestone used in construction, and it can still be seen standing on the edge of the desert.

The Red Pyramid was a wonderful achievement, but shortly afterwards it was eclipsed by an even bigger pyramid that was constructed a few miles to the north, on the Giza plateau. This was the Great Pyramid of Khufu. It stood 481 feet high and the base covered 13 acres. It is the only one of the Seven Wonders of the Ancient World that has survived until today.

Two other pharaohs, Khafre ("KAF-rah") and Menkaure ("men-KOW-rah"), also built their tombs at Giza, but these pyramids were less ambitious.

The Old Kingdom was also a time for great exploration. Nubia to the south was conquered, mining expeditions were sent to the Sinai, and fleets of ships sailed to the Phoenician coast to bring back the highly prized cedar wood.

After the fifth dynasty there appears to have been a power struggle between the pharaohs and the noblemen. We see the tombs of rich lords becoming more elaborate, while the workmanship on the pharaohs' pyramids declines. By the end of the sixth dynasty, the monarchy collapsed altogether, and the Old Kingdom came to an end.

A painted relief in a tomb in Sakkara shows subjects bringing gifts, a practice common in ancient Egypt.

THE MIDDLE KINGDOM

For nearly a hundred years Egypt entered a dark age. No mining took place, no new temples were constructed, and the country lacked any central government.

It was Mentuhotep who seized control of the country and established the twelfth dynasty. Under his rule, and that of other strong kings who followed, Egypt's power and wealth was restored.

The badly neglected irrigation system was repaired, and many new projects undertaken. Nubia was reconquered, and Senwosret III built a string of forts to secure Egypt's southern border. A large Egyptian army was sent into Palestine, most likely to protect Egypt's increasingly important trade links with the region. During the Middle Kingdom, Egyptian ships even reached places as far away as Syria, Crete and Greece.

It was a golden period for art and literature, with many new ideas being introduced. There was some beautiful royal sculpture produced, and wonderful wooden models of soldiers, houses and animals were placed in tombs. The pharaohs of the Middle Kingdom continued to build pyramids almost as large as the Great Pyramids of the Old Kingdom, although less expensive building materials were used.

By 1640 B.C., Egypt was again facing serious problems with which weaker kings proved unable to cope. Immigrants who had been settling in the Delta started to become a powerful political force. They had more advanced weapons than the Egyptians, including horse-drawn chariots. As a result of this military superiority, their leaders, known as the Hyksos Kings, were able to seize control of the Delta. For nearly a century they ruled a large section of Egypt.

THE NEW KINGDOM

In time the Egyptians were able to acquire the same weapons as the Hyksos tribes. This enabled Ahmose, the King of southern Egypt, to drive the invaders out of the Delta. Ahmose retained his capital at Thebes, which now became the most important city in Egypt.

During the New Kingdom, Egypt kept a large permanent army, with its own elite chariot regiments. Under a series of warrior kings they undertook a more aggressive foreign policy that soon made them the dominant force throughout the near east. Kings and local rulers from as far away as Syria paid homage to the great pharaoh in Egypt. With gold, copper, ivory, ebony and slaves pouring into the land, Egypt became richer than ever before. Thutmose I was one of the greatest of the warrior pharaohs, and he also pioneered a new style of royal burial in "The Valley of the Kings."

The reign of Amenhotep IV threw Egypt into religious turmoil. He believed in a single god called Aton, who was represented by the disk of the sun. He changed his name to Akhenaton and built a new capital city.

The temple of Ramses II at Abu Simbel has four 70-foot high statues of the King. At the foot of the statues are his mother, his chief wife and eight of his 140 children, shown on a much smaller scale. Apart from his military campaigns, Ramses II also put an enormous amount of the country's energy into building great temples and monuments.

THE MISSING PHARAOH

Tutankhamen was probably no more than ten years old when he came to the throne. We know very little about the young king, except that he reigned for around eight years, and probably died from a head wound caused by a spear or arrow. Compared with many other kings, Tutankhamen had a short and uneventful reign—yet by accident he was to become the most famous pharaoh of all.

Buried in the Valley of the Kings, his existence was forgotten for three thousand years until 1922, when an Englishman, Howard Carter, after years of searching for the missing tomb, made the greatest archeological find of all time. Together with the Pharaoh were discovered thousands of items that had been buried with him, including gold jewelry, statues, thrones, beds, and a golden face mask. There were also bunches of dried flowers, picked fresh the day the king had been buried. We can only wonder who placed this touching gift amongst all the gold and finery.

In the battle of Kadesh, Hittite chariots swept down on Ramses II's army of Nubians, catching them unawares. But the Egyptians rallied strongly and the battle ended any hopes either side had of victory.

This was a wonderful period for artists, architects and poets, who were all given freedom to experiment. However, rivalry between Akhenaton and the priests of the old religion soon brought civil unrest to the country. Egypt's domestic problems—plus Akhenaton's hatred of war—in turn led to the loss of its Asian empire.

The new religion quickly died out after Akhenaton's death. His successor, King Tutankhamen, was forced by the priests to return to the worship of the old religion.

During the late New Kingdom, Seti I ("SEH-tee") and Ramses II launched military campaigns to regain Egypt's lost influence in Asia, but by now new forces had risen in the area. Ramses assembled the biggest army Egypt had ever seen, but was lucky to avoid a shattering defeat at the hands of the Hittites. These were a mixed group of people whose capital was in central Turkey. The lesson of this campaign was that Egypt would never again be the one great superpower in the world.

EGYPT INVADED

After the twentieth dynasty, which ended around 1070 B.C., Egypt went into a rapid decline. Nubians, Assyrians and Persians each conquered the country to found their own short-lived line of kings.

In 332 B.C., Alexander the Great swept out of Macedonia with his mighty army and made Egypt part of his vast empire. He only stayed in Egypt for a few months, but in that short time founded the city of Alexandria. After his death, Egypt came under the control of a general called Ptolemy who founded the Ptolemaic dynasty. At first Egypt fared well under Greek rule and the new capital of Alexandria became a great city of trade and culture.

Queen Cleopatra was the last of the Ptolemy rulers, and she found herself caught up in the politics of the Roman Empire that was now dominating the Mediterranean. She married Mark Anthony, co-ruler of Rome, in an alliance against his great rival, Octavian. However, their combined fleets were defeated at the Battle of Actium, and the following year— by which time their position had become hopeless—they committed suicide.

Egypt now came under the rule of Rome, who wanted little from the land except wheat to feed the great Roman Empire. However, the Romans, like the Greeks before them, were content to leave the Egyptians their own ancient religion. That changed with the arrival of Christianity, and from A.D. 600 onwards Egypt was rapidly converted to a Christian country.

The 7th century saw a dynamic force emerge in the region as Arab warriors set out to conquer the world in the name of their new Islamic religion. Egypt fell to the Arabs in A.D. 639, and they established a small fortress town that was to soon grow into the great city of Cairo.

Above: **Ancient ruins of Alexandria—a reminder of the glory of a vanished era.**

Below: **A coin portrait of Greek conqueror, Alexander the Great. Under Greek rule, Egyptian arts and trade flourished.**

THE GOLDEN AGE

The Arabs influenced the lives of the ordinary people of Egypt more than any of the earlier conquerors. The Arabic language became widely spoken, and the majority of people elected to convert from Christianity to Islam. Egypt was now governed by Moslem leaders known as caliphs, and was usually part of a larger empire. First the Umayyad dynasty ruled the country from their capital at Damascus, then Egypt came under the jurisdiction of the Baghdad-based Abbasid dynasty. From A.D. 868 to 969, two Turkish dynasties, the Tulunid and Ikhshidid, ruled Egypt with only token acknowledgment of Baghdad's overall authority.

In the 12th century, Egypt became caught up in the struggle for the control of Jerusalem. Crusader forces from Europe invaded the coast of Egypt and the Fatimid rulers asked the Caliph of Syria in 1169 to send them military assistance. An army officer called Saladin commanded the forces that defeated the Crusaders, but he also overthrew the Fatimid rulers and made himself prince of Egypt. He returned Egypt to the orthodox, Sunni religion, and became a hero of the Moslem world by driving the Crusaders out of Jerusalem.

The descendants of Saladin employed a group of slaves known as the Mamluks ("mam-LUKE") for their bodyguards. Because of their loyalty, they quickly rose to high positions in the government and army. In 1250, they were strong enough to rebel and seize Egypt for themselves. Even after the Mamluks were overthrown by the Ottoman Turks in 1517, they continued to act as governors and often seemed to hold more power than their Turkish masters.

The Ibn Tulun Mosque is the oldest mosque in Cairo. It was built by Ibn Tulun, who was sent to Egypt by the Abbasid Caliph in 868, to act as governor. Later, Ibn Tulun established his own dynasty, taking advantage of a weakening Abbasid government.

Mohammed Ali (1769-1849) was a dynamic leader who initiated Egypt's first modernization program. He created new ministries and schools, built canals, introduced cotton to the country and developed a textile industry. By the time of his death, Egypt had acquired an international standing.

THE EUROPEANS ARRIVE

During the 16th and 17th centuries Egypt became a forgotten corner of the world. However, in 1798, the country was dramatically returned to the world stage when it was invaded by a large French army under Napoleon Bonaparte. It was his ambition to found a French colony and disrupt England's communications with her empire in India.

Such hopes were destroyed with the defeat of the French navy at the hands of the British fleet of Admiral Nelson. The following year, Napoleon left his army and returned to France. Without Napoleon's inspiration the French forces were driven out of Egypt by the Ottomans and their allies.

As in the time of Saladin, an army officer sent to aid Egypt from outside forces again took the opportunity to take power for himself. In this case, it was a young Turkish officer called Mohammed Ali. He proved to be a remarkable ruler, who worked hard to modernize the country, and under his guidance Egypt established much closer contacts with the West.

In 1859, France was granted a contract to build a canal through the isthmus of Suez. The building of the Suez Canal was to make Egypt strategically important to the great European powers. From then onwards, Egypt was to be increasingly vulnerable to political events in other parts of the world. Lavish spending by its rulers put Egypt into debt, and in 1875 they sold their shares in the canal to Britain. British influence in Egypt grew so powerful that they were soon interfering in Egypt's domestic issues.

Anti-British uprisings in 1880 and 1882 led to a British military invasion. Although Egypt had a king and was still part of the Turkish Empire, it was the British administrators which now held the real power. In areas such as banking the British made some excellent reforms, but they neglected education and public health, and an increasingly strong independence movement developed.

Tombstones at Al Ala-
mein, monument to the
war dead. The Battle of
Al Alamein in 1942 was a
crucial turning point in
World War II as it halted
the combined German
and Italian advance on
Suez.

THE STRUGGLE FOR INDEPENDENCE

In 1914, the Great War broke out in Europe. When Turkey sided with
Germany, Britain declared Egypt a protectorate and sent a large number of
troops to guard the Suez Canal. This created more anti-British feeling and
the nationalist movement, led by Saad Zaghlul, became increasingly
powerful. In 1922, Britain granted Egypt independence, but still retained
the right to station troops in the country.

The Second World War once again saw Egypt involved in European
politics, and this time the country became a major battlefield for foreign
armies. German forces invaded Egypt in an attempt to capture the Suez
Canal and the Middle East oil fields. At one point they were only a hundred
miles from the Nile Delta, but were defeated at the Battle of Al Alamein.
Throughout the war, Egypt was a major British base, and hundreds of
thousands of troops passed through the country.

Egypt emerged from the war all the more determined to remove foreign
influence from the country. In 1945, they became a founding member of the
United Nations and were involved in the formation of the Arab League.

In 1948, Palestine was divided into Jewish and Arab states, and Egypt became involved in the war with Israel.

Their defeat fueled a growing feeling of discontent, and in July 1952, a group of army officers seized power. King Farouk was sent into exile, and the country became a republic. Shortly after the revolution, Gamal Abdel Nasser replaced Mohammed Naguib as president, and started to tackle Egypt's serious social problems. A major reform was the Land Act which broke up the big estates and gave land to the fellahin ("fel-lah-HEEN"), Egypt's farm laborers. On the international scene, Nasser negotiated a withdrawal of all British troops, to be completed by June 1956.

A leading member of the revolution which overthrew the monarchy in 1952, Nasser introduced many reforms when he became Egypt's president. Among his accomplishments were the building of the Aswan Dam and the modernization of the country.

Nasser also dreamed of building a new dam at Aswan, and had expected the Western powers to assist with the project. When they refused, Egypt seized control of the Suez Canal, intending to use the tolls to pay for the dam. In October 1956, Egypt was invaded by Israel, and the following month Britain and France landed troops in the Canal Zone and captured Port Said. Although Egypt could not defeat the European powers on the battlefield, world opinion forced the Anglo-French forces to withdraw.

The Suez invasion left Nasser as a powerful figure in both regional and world politics. In 1958, he was asked to enter Egypt into a political union with Syria, and to become president of a new country called the United Arab Republic. Such a union was never really likely to succeed, and Syria withdrew in 1961. Egypt, however, retained the title United Arab Republic until 1971.

The years following World War II saw Egypt emerge as an independent country, ready to take a central place on the world stage. However, Egypt and Israel remained hostile toward each other, and this relationship was to dominate events for the next two decades.

GOVERNMENT

UNTIL THE 1950s, Egypt was a constitutional monarchy ruled by a king. However, social conditions, and a disastrous war with Israel, caused considerable discontent. In July 1952, a group of army officers took power. King Farouk was sent into exile, and the following year Egypt became a republic.

At first, the new government adopted a socialist policy, and close ties were built up with Russia. However, under President Anwar el-Sadat, Egypt shifted closer to the West, and adopted a more open economic policy. In the last few years Egypt has granted her people more political freedoms.

THE ROLE OF THE PRESIDENT

Since the revolution of 1952, Egypt has been a republic, ruled by a president. The president must be Egyptian, born of Egyptian parents, and be at least forty years old. The president is elected for a six-year period, after which he can then serve additional terms. Two of Egypt's four presidents have remained in power until their deaths.

President Naguib headed the country immediately after the revolution but soon found himself arguing with his council. He was replaced in November 1954 by President Nasser. Nasser remained president until his sudden death from heart attack in 1970. President Sadat then took office until he was assassinated in 1981. Hosni Mubarak has been president since then.

Only one person can run for president, and he must be nominated by at least two-thirds of Egypt's legislature and be elected by the majority of them. His nomination is then taken to the people who must approve him in a public referendum. Both Sadat and Mubarak were already serving as vice-president when they were nominated.

Above: **The first Arabic leader to visit Israel, Sadat was awarded the 1978 Nobel Prize for Peace, jointly with Prime Minister Menachem Begin of Israel. In 1981, he was gunned down by Moslem fundamentalists at a military parade.**

Opposite: **The monument to Anwar el-Sadat.**

The president has enormous power:

• He appoints and dismisses the prime minister and his deputies, and the ministers and their deputies. He can also appoint one or more vice-presidents.

• Together with the cabinet that he has appointed, he defines the general state policy and oversees its implementation.

• He is the supreme commander of the armed forces, and when necessary, declares war, having sought the approval of the legislative body (People's Assembly).

• He calls a referendum of the people on matters of supreme importance relating to the country's interest.

One of Sadat's most trusted colleagues, Hosni Mubarak took over the presidency of Egypt after the former's death. He has proved a hardworking and popular president. Under his guidance, there has been a relaxation of control at home while Egypt has rebuilt its ties with the Arabic world. In 1987, President Mubarak was re-elected for a second term of office.

GOVERNMENT

The government is the supreme executive and administrative body in Egypt. The cabinet is composed of the prime minister, his deputies and the ministers. The government is headed by the prime minister. The main tasks of the government are to guide, coordinate and oversee the running of the ministries as well as issue decrees, draft new laws, and draw up the general budget and general state plan.

Egypt also has an elected legislature called the People's Assembly. It has 454 seats of which 444 are elected, and ten are appointed by the president. The president normally uses his seats to ensure that the Coptic minority are represented. Members of the assembly hold office for six years and at least half the assembly must be workers and farmers. In theory, it is a powerful body with considerable power: it supervises the executive authority, approves the general state policy and budget, and is entitled to propose laws. However, in practice, the assembly often does little more than approve the president's decisions.

Supporting all sections of the government is the Shura Council. The Shura does not have any authority, but is a respected advisory body. The council serves for six years, with half the members changing every three years. The last council was formed in 1989 and had ten women members. It considers matters such as the constitution, new laws, or any policy referred to it by the president.

At regional level, Egypt is divided into 26 governorates (provinces), each with a governor who is appointed by the president. The governor works alongside an elected council and has considerable power. He will make decisions such as the building of a new hospital or school. Below the level of governors come district and village mayors, with their own elected councils.

THE FLAG

The Egyptian flag has a complicated history. Prior to 1914, Egypt was part of the Ottoman Empire and flew the Turkish flag. However, Mohammed Ali had his own flag, with three crescents, and this "royal" banner became the official Egyptian flag after 1914. During the independence struggle, a green flag with a crescent and cross was often flown. The symbols showed that both Moslems and Christians supported the fight for independence. It was a variation of this flag that was used after independence was achieved in 1922.

The present Egyptian flag was first hoisted after the 1952 revolution and was based on the Arab Liberation flag. The white stands for the country's bright future, the black for the dark past, and the red for the revolution. The hawk emblem is associated with Mohammed, the founder of Islam.

Monument at Aswan High Dam commemorates the friendship between Egypt and the Soviet Union. The High Dam was completed with Soviet help when the Western powers refused to assist with the project.

FOREIGN POLICY

For the last fifty years, Egypt's foreign policy has been dominated by her relationship with Israel. As a leader of the Arabic world, Egypt was initially hostile to the Israeli state and wished to see the land returned to the Palestinian people. In 1967, President Nasser entered a military alliance with Syria and Jordan and closed the Gulf of Aqaba to Israeli shipping. It is possible that this was a preliminary step before the launching of an attack.

The Israelis certainly believed so, and on June 5, 1967, they launched a mass attack of their own. Virtually the entire Egyptian air force was destroyed on the ground, and Egypt was totally defeated in the Six-Day War that followed. Her army was shattered, the Sinai was in Israeli hands and the Suez Canal was closed.

After this crushing defeat, President Nasser offered his resignation but mass public support persuaded him to stay. The USSR took advantage of the situation to gain influence in the Middle East, and provided millions of dollars worth of military equipment to rebuild the Egyptian army. After several border incidents that threatened to resume the war, the United States and the United Nations arranged a cease-fire.

However, with Egyptian territory in Israeli hands, there could be no real peace. After the sudden death of Nasser, Sadat became president. In October 1973, he ordered an attack on Israel. In a daring move, Egyptian troops stormed the fortifications along the Suez Canal and quickly overran the Sinai. For a while, complete victory looked possible. However, the Israeli army, resupplied with a massive airlift by the United States, were able to strike back and regain much of the ground they had lost.

The war may not have ended in a decisive victory, but Egypt had destroyed the myth of Israeli superiority and gained a new confidence and dignity from their performance in the war. As a result of this, Egypt now felt strong enough to seek peace. In 1975, Israel returned part of the Sinai, and in 1977, President Sadat made a historic visit to Jerusalem to address the Israeli Knesset (Parliament). Later, Egypt and Israel signed the Camp David Accord, which saw Israel return the rest of the Sinai, and the two countries concluded a formal peace treaty in 1979. This was the first treaty between Israel and any Arab nation.

In October 1973, Egyptian forces stormed the fortifications along the Suez Canal in a surprise assault on the Sinai. The success of this operation enabled President Sadat to open peace talks with Israel on an advantageous basis.

The rest of the Arab world was furious at what they saw as President Sadat's betrayal, and broke off relationships with Egypt. Some Egyptians also felt the government had given away too much, but many supported the move. However, in 1981, President Sadat was assassinated by a group of extremists who were opposed to his policies.

Under President Mubarak, Egypt has continued to maintain diplomatic ties with Israel, and has moved closer to the United States and the Western world. By the 1980s Egypt was more concerned about its western border, where relationships with Libya were becoming increasingly hostile. In 1989, Egypt rejoined the Arab League, but the 1990 Gulf Crisis again saw Egypt involved in a military adventure within the region. After President Mubarak had failed in his attempts to mediate a settlement, Egypt sent 30,000 troops and two armored divisions to help free Kuwait.

ECONOMY

FARMING is still the most important section of the economy. It is true that oil has now overtaken agriculture as Egypt's major source of foreign earnings. However, the oil industry only employs a small number of Egyptians compared to farming. In addition, the price of oil can fluctuate drastically, leaving the economy volatile and liable to depression.

Since the peace settlement with Israel, Egypt has been able to develop its tourist industry, which is now a major earner of foreign exchange. The Suez Canal has also reopened and the toll fees make another major contribution to the economy.

AGRICULTURE

Egypt has approximately six million acres of land under cultivation. Although other sections of the economy have now overtaken it as a money earner, farming still provides much of the country's food needs, and keeps millions of people employed. For these reasons agriculture can still be considered as the central structure of the economy. It was hoped that the building of the high dam would allow more land to be reclaimed from the desert. Some projects have been very successful, but at the same time good farmland around the Nile has been built on to meet the housing needs of the growing population. As a result, the total amount of land under cultivation has not increased as much as had been predicted.

Because Egypt has virtually no rain, all crops depend on irrigation. Egypt has been taking water from the Nile since pharaonic times, and some of these ancient methods are still practiced today. However, an increasing amount of water is being pumped from the Nile with the help of modern machines. Once water is provided, Egypt's days of endless sunshine usually ensure an excellent crop.

Above: **Orange pickers. Agriculture in Egypt is done more on a commercial rather than subsistence basis. It contributes one-fourth of the country's GNP (Gross National Product), and employs almost three-fifths of its population.**

Opposite: **All farmlands in Egypt must be irrigated with water from the Nile or subterranean wells. Here, a donkey pumps water from a well using an age-old device.**

Harvested sugarcane being loaded onto a truck. Besides sugarcane, a wide range of vegetables and cereal crops, such as wheat, barley, potatoes, beans, rice and onions is produced for home consumption and export.

Most land will give two crops a year. Barley, wheat and beans are typical summer crops, while winter crops might include rice, corn or sorghum. Egyptian clover, known as berseem, is grown throughout the year as animal feed.

Before the 1952 land reforms, much of the countryside was in the hands of rich landowners. After the revolution, the big farms were broken into small units and given to the fellahin. On some of the land the government reserved the right to say what crops would be grown, and to purchase these crops at set prices. As government prices have generally been low, it has not motivated farmers to produce good harvests. This problem has been recognized, and now there are only three crops that must still be sold to the government. These are cotton, sugarcane and half the rice crop.

The fact that the land is broken up by thousands of irrigation canals

IRRIGATING THE LAND

Ancient methods of irrigation are still employed in Egypt. These include the *shadoof* which is perhaps the simplest method of all. It consists of a bucket at the end of a long pole that is dipped into the water and counterbalanced with large stones.

The *sakiya* is a vertical waterwheel with buckets or pots fixed onto it. These vessels collect water on the way up, and drop it into a small canal on the way down. Such a wheel is driven by a donkey or buffalo.

The Archimedean screw is an ancient but ingenious invention. When turned, the screw action forces water through the tube. An Archimedean screw can water three quarters of an acre of land a day.

means that many fields are relatively small. This has made it difficult to introduce modern farming methods. This, plus the fellahin's resistance to change, means that much of the work on the land is still done by human or animal labor.

The land the government has newly reclaimed from the desert has not been so dictated by tradition, and some of the more exciting experiments have taken place here. New crops have also been experimented with, such as strawberries and high quality vegetables for export.

Cotton, however, remains the main cash crop. Cotton was brought to Egypt by Mohammed Ali, and the country was able to acquire a large share of the world market when the southern states were placed under siege during the American Civil War. Today, cotton accounts for nearly one fifth of Egypt's export earnings, and provides the base for the domestic spinning and weaving industry.

Iron ore, mined in the Western Desert, provides the raw material for Egypt's iron and steel processing industries.

INDUSTRY

After the revolution, President Nasser made a policy of encouraging industry. Thus, most Egyptian factories are still either owned or supervised by the government. This has caused problems, for many state factories are poorly managed and over-staffed. As a result, they are often run at a loss. There is a move to privatize some industries, but this is likely to be a slow process.

Despite the problems, manufacturing now accounts for nearly one fifth of the country's production. Most of the Egyptian industries are "agro-allied," which means they make direct use of agricultural produce. Textile production, using Egyptian cotton, and food processing are the most important industries.

However, the government has made a policy of opening up different types of factories, and hopes to make Egypt less dependent on imports. A major project was the building of the Helwan Steel Works, with a direct rail link to the iron ore mine in the Western Desert. This has enabled a heavy industrial program to develop, and much of Egypt's armament industry has been built at Helwan to take advantage of the steel works. Other factories have preferred to be based at Alexandria for convenient use of the international port.

Egypt has several cement plants, which can meet half its needs, but the balance still has to be imported. There are major fertilizer plants at Tukla and El Dikheila, and an important aluminum plant at Nag Hammadi.

Recently, Egypt has been trying to develop non-traditional exports such as shoes, clothing and fresh agricultural produce. However, many of these goods were once sold to the Soviet Union and east European nations.

Textiles, in all hues and colors, can be found in many of the Egyptian shops and markets. First developed by Mohammed Ali, Egypt's textile production has become a major manufacturing industry.

Changes in that part of the world have seriously reduced the market.

Despite the growing number of factories, Egypt still has to import many items. In addition to food, the major imports are transportation goods and machinery, chemicals, wood, paper and metal products. Indeed, each year, Egypt buys more than it can sell, causing a worrying trade deficit.

OIL

Oil was first discovered in Egypt in 1938, but only in small quantities. It is only in the last thirty years that oil production has become an important part of the Egyptian economy. Even with the present relatively low price per barrel, oil still accounts for 55% of Egyptian export earnings. Equally important is the fact that having its own oil has made Egypt economically and politically independent of its Arabic neighbors.

All oil activity is controlled by the state-owned Egyptian General Petroleum Corporation. However much of the exploration and production work is completed by foreign firms who keep a share of the oil.

The main Egyptian oil fields are located in the Gulf of Suez, although the relatively small Al Alamayn field in the Western Desert is also producing. Ninety percent of Egyptian oil comes from offshore.

Once the oil is ashore, Egypt has good handling facilities. There are six major refineries in Egypt and several important pipelines. The largest is the Suez to Mediterranean pipeline that takes oil from the eastern fields to the refinery at Alexandria.

Gasoline is heavily subsidized in Egypt, and home demand is increasing rapidly. In 1990, it was estimated that Egypt produced 850,000 barrels of oil a day. Out of this, 450,000 barrels were used domestically, and after the foreign partners took their share only 200,000 barrels were left for export. Despite its oil reserves, Egypt may soon find itself becoming an oil importer.

Most of Egypt's oil comes from offshore. The wells are drilled by oil rigs such as this, off the coast of the Sinai.

Raising the price of gasoline could help conserve stocks, but such a move would affect all aspects of agricultural and industrial production, and be extremely unpopular.

Exploration is continuing, and in the 1980s, Egypt brought 1,200 new wells into production. However, while new wells are being found, they are generally of small size. It is estimated that Egyptian oil will only last another twenty years if extracted from the ground at the present rate.

One promising area is natural gas. Egypt has two major gas fields at Abu Gharadiq and Abu Maadi, and it has only just started to exploit these. It is hoped that increased use of natural gas might slow down Egypt's oil demand. The country is also hoping to obtain more energy from coal-fired and gas-powered electric generating stations.

TOURISM

Tourism is the second most important sector of the economy after oil. Egypt was one of the first nations to develop an important tourist trade, and during the days of steamship travel passengers sailing through the Suez Canal would often make a detour to visit the pyramids. In those days, it was a great adventure to journey out of Cairo to Giza, and the trip would take a full day by camel or donkey. Today, the same journey takes less than an hour in a luxury bus.

The modern tourist industry is well developed, and there is a good range of hotels of all standards. Air Egypt and other smaller domestic airlines carry passengers quickly between the capital and the temples of the far south. Once on the ground there are fleets of modern coaches to move visitors from one site to the next.

Tourism is an ideal industry for Egypt. It employs many people, and brings in vital foreign exchange. The tourist industry is based around Cairo and Luxor. Most visitors to Cairo wish to see the pyramids and the National Museum with its wonderful Tutankhamen collection.

Although many people come to Egypt to see the pharaonic ruins, there are also other attractions. The Sinai has become a popular area for snorkeling and diving vacations. People also visit Mount Catherine monastery and climb Mount Sinai. There are many other possibilities for walking holidays in this wild region which could be developed.

Unfortunately the tourist industry is always vulnerable to outside events. The hijacking of the 1980s and the 1991 Gulf War had a drastic effect on the tourist industry. These events caused a loss of vital revenue for Egypt, and hardship to the many people who have come to depend on the trade.

A tour guide explains the significance of a temple painting to a group of tourists. Tourism is a major source of revenue for the Egyptian government. In addition to the people directly employed in the industry, a great number make their living on the fringe. These include camel owners who give rides, people who work in the tourist shops and even young boys who wait around the major sites hoping to be employed as unofficial guides.

EGYPTIANS

AROUND 80% OF EGYPT'S POPULATION are Hamitic Arabs, which means a combination of the ancient Egyptian Hamite people and the Arabs who moved into the land from the 7th century onward. However, there have been many other influences. There are some very dark skinned Egyptians who have traces of Nubian blood in them. There are also much lighter skinned people who are of Turkish descent. There are even some blond haired Egyptians, who have a Syrian background.

Despite this mixture, there are facial features that would be recognized as "typically Egyptian." Although Egypt is categorized as an Arabic nation, many Egyptians are proud of their own unique history and culture, and consider themselves different from the rest of the Arabic world.

The fellahin living in the countryside generally marry within their village, and so have mixed less with other races than city people. As a result, they can be considered the direct descendants of the ancient Egyptians. Egypt also has a large population of Coptic Christians. They also tend to avoid intermarrying with other groups, and often claim an even more direct descent from the ancient Egyptians than their Moslem neighbors.

Egypt also has two clearly recognizable minorities, the Nubians and the Bedouins. The Nubians come from the deep south of the country, although since the building of the High Dam they have become more widely dispersed. The Bedouins were originally desert nomads. Today, however, many of them live in villages in the oases.

The oasis people are not usually considered a minority group, but they differ from the people of the Nile in their hereditary background and culture. Although Moslems, and of Berber and Arabic stock, they have a life-style and customs not shared by any other section of Egyptian society.

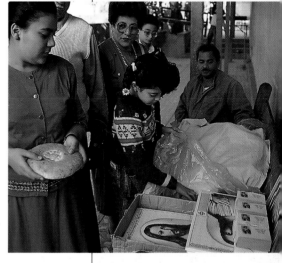

Above: **Coptic Christians buy communion bread outside a church. Comprising 15% of Egypt's population, the Copts are mostly found in Asyut, Luxor, Cairo and Alexandria.**

Opposite: **A fellahin with a "typically Egyptian" look.**

FELLAHIN

Three fifths of Egypt's population still make their living from the land. These rural farmers of the Nile Valley and Delta are known as fellahin. The name comes from the Arabic word *falaha*, which means to labor or till the earth.

Many fellahin are of stocky build, of average or short height. Over the centuries they have only occasionally intermarried with Negro and Arabic people, and so retain a distinctive "Egyptian" look. The majority of fellahin live in small villages of between 1,000 and 5,000 people. Individual houses are most likely to be simple one-story buildings, with thick walls made of unbaked mud bricks, although today many rural houses are being made from cement blocks. The family probably keeps goats, chickens, sheep and buffaloes, and the animals are kept inside the yard at night.

Described by President Nasser as the "true" Egyptians, the fellahin live close to the land, and rely on it for their livelihood. Many fellahin, such as the one above, use animals to help them in their work.

The lives of the fellahin might appear to have changed little for hundreds of years. Certainly if you were to look at pictures of farming on the walls of ancient tombs, you would notice a remarkable similarity with scenes that still go on in the countryside today. However, the basic standard of living has improved in the last 40 years. Medicine is a prime example, and basic health care now reaches most villages. Virtually every community has a central well or fountain that provides clean, piped water.

Electricity is also finding its way into the villages, while radios—and to a lesser extent television—are making the fellahin more aware of events both in Egypt and the outside world. Before the revolution, the only schools were those run by the mosques. Today, virtually every child has at least the opportunity to attend a government school.

Whether in the cities or in the rural areas, Egyptians are a passionate people, proud of their heritage. If asked, they usually describe themselves as "Egyptian" and seldom as "Arabic."

THE EGYPTIAN CHARACTER

The Egyptian character has largely been shaped by the environment and traditions of the village. Life in the countryside was very hard, so people were always ready to help each other. This has become one national characteristic, and somebody in trouble in Cairo today—whether lost or in an accident—is likely to be surrounded by people trying to help.

The Egyptians are remarkably resilient, and they seem to have the ability to stay cheerful in the face of great ill fortune or bad news. This is perhaps the result of centuries of enduring suffering and poverty. Yet, at the same time, they can be extremely excitable people, ready to argue and shout over small everyday matters. Fortunately, they are usually just as quick to embrace and forgive.

Egyptians have a strong sense of humor. Jests and practical jokes are greeted with loud infectious laughter. Political jokes are popular, and often very clever, but any subject can be made something to laugh about. Like many nationalities they have a group they often make fun of, and city people have a large collection of jokes about the fellahin. Yet, at the same time, many city people admire and respect the country people for their common sense and stubbornness.

Perhaps the single most uniting factor for all Egyptians is their pride in their country, in the "Egyptian way" and in the Egyptian soil. All Egyptians, even those living in cities, consider themselves "people of the land."

A Bedouin woman in the Sinai gathers wood to make a fire. Many Bedouin tribes were driven out of the Sinai during the 1973 war, and took refuge in the cities. Some groups built shacks along canals on the outskirts of Cairo, and have never returned to the desert.

THE BEDOUINS

The Bedouins form the most distinct tribe within Egypt. They live in the Western Desert or Sinai, where they were traditionally nomads, moving their flocks from one oasis to the next. They have a reputation of being proud, temperamental, independent and, above all hospitable people.

Camels are an important part of the Bedouins' life. Apart from transportation they can be milked, and the molted hair used for making clothing, tents and carpets. Bedouin cuisine has been shaped by the limitations of their desert life, and lamb and rice form a large part of the diet. Meals are generally eaten in silence, the men dining in a separate tent from the women.

Families might supplement their income with rug weaving or handicrafts. The rugs are made on small looms and vary in style and color from tribe to tribe. Bedouin jewelry is made from silver or base metal, and is often large and heavy. Rings, earrings and necklaces are the favorite pieces.

Although traditionally romanticized, desert life is in fact extremely hard, and today many Bedouin people have adopted a more settled lifestyle. It has been the policy of the Egyptian government to provide the Bedouins with medical centers and schools, and so encourage them to settle. Some families have become date farmers, while young men often seek work in the Sinai oil fields or on construction projects. This income has brought changes to the lifestyle, and cars and trucks now play a great part in the life of the villages.

THE NUBIANS

The Nubians come from the deep south of Egypt. Although they have Arabic blood, they have their own unique racial characteristics. Nubians tend to be tall, thin and dark skinned. Many Nubian women have decorative patterns tattooed on their lips. Within Egypt, the Nubian people have a reputation for hospitality. Today, the Nubians probably number around 50,000.

Nubian homes are made of clay and straw bricks baked hard in the sun. Both the inside and outside of the homes are usually decorated with murals of trees, boats and sacred symbols. These paintings are done with the fingers rather than with brushes. Porcelain plates brought from Cairo might also be inserted into the walls.

Nubian villagers do their shopping at a local market near Kom Ombo, a re-settlement area.

The Nubian economy has always been based on date growing, which not only produced food but provided timber and ropes. Since the building of the High Dam, the Nubians have had to move out of their traditional land to be resettled in new areas. Attempts to introduce them to different types of farming have generally not been successful, as Nubian culture has no experience of such work. Many Nubian men travel into Egyptian cities to seek work, but family ties remain strong and they usually return to their home village once they have earned sufficient money. Such a labor migration has been going on long before the building of the dam and is not necessarily the result of recent changes.

الصف الأول
٢/١

Pupils of an oasis wait patiently for class to start. The original inhabitants of the oases were primarily of Berber stock, and the strain still survives in the lighter coloring of many of them.

PEOPLE OF THE OASES

The people who live in the oases were originally of Berber stock, but now have many other influences. For example, Kharijah oasis was on the great caravan route, and has many dark skinned people of African decent. Whatever their racial mix, the oasis dwellers tend to see themselves as being different from the people of the Nile.

Certainly in the remote oasis of Siwa there are significant differences in customs, dress and language. Siwa has a population of around 10,000, and the people are a mixture of Berber, Bedouin and Sudanese. Siwa women lead very restricted lives. If they leave their homes, they generally wear a square of grey woolen cloth that covers them from head to foot. Many women are not permitted to leave the homes at all, and Siwa is one of the few communities where the men take on the work of fetching water. Young girls, however, may wear brightly embroidered dresses. Siwa wedding dresses are particularly famed for their elaborate work.

Siwa food is basically the same as that found in most of Egypt, but with a heavy Bedouin influence. Lamb is widely used.

THE TRIBES OF THE EASTERN DESERT

Twenty years ago, nobody believed that any tribes lived in the Eastern Desert. The region was thought to be too hostile an environment to support human life. However, we now know that two tribes, the Ababdah and the Bisharin, do survive here. These tribes belong to a larger group of people known as the Beja group, who live between the Nile Valley and Red Sea, as far south as Ethiopia. The Ababdah live in the area immediately south of Aswan, while the Bisharin occupy the southwest corner of Egypt, extending into the Sudan. Both tribes speak a language called *To Bedawi*, although most Ababdah and some Bisharin men also know Arabic.

A majority of the sedentary population of the Eastern Desert live in settlements, trading or herding camels, goats and sheep for a living.

Some members of both tribes still live a traditional nomadic life in the inner desert, and they call themselves the "Mountain People." They live in small cocoon-shaped dwellings made of tree branches and covered with rugs. These can be packed up and taken to the next spot as the tribe moves on in the search for food and water.

Few people anywhere on our planet live in such isolation from the rest of the world. The only outside contact the Mountain People have is with former nomadic tribes now living in settlements on the desert edge. People from these settlements act as traders for the Mountain People, taking their animals to market and bringing back flour, sugar, coffee, gold and silver.

The Ababdah and Bisharin tend to be small, dark and muscular. The women wear gold or silver jewelry and wrap themselves in colorful cloth. The men hang charms around their necks, and wear daggers attached by leather straps to their arms.

PEOPLE, PEOPLE, EVERYWHERE

Egypt is in the middle of an enormous population explosion. A million people are added to the population every nine months. That is the equivalent of a baby being born about every 23 seconds.

This uncontrolled population growth is putting a tremendous strain on a country that is not only poor, but which has less than 4% of its area suitable for habitation. The dangers were evident thirty years ago, when President Nasser described Egypt's greatest concern as "the 1,000 new Egyptians born every day."

Already the country has to import vast amounts of food just to feed itself. There is no longer enough land to divide up, and many young men are being forced into the cities to seek work. This not only strains the infrastructure of the urban areas, but breaks up the traditional Egyptian family ties. The medical, education and transportation systems are all struggling to meet the new demands.

THE GALABIA—THE NATIONAL DRESS

In Egyptian villages, the most common costume for men is the galabia, which resembles an ankle-length nightshirt. It has long, loose sleeves and a round neck. The winter galabia is made from flannel or heavy cotton but the summer galabia is lighter. They are generally in dull colors.

Underneath, the men wear cotton shirts and shorts. When working in the fields, they may remove their galabia and work in their underclothing. Some men, particularly the more elderly, wear a woolen skull cap. The galabia is very much an Egyptian dress, and is generally not used by other people in the Middle East.

A black galabia-type costume is common dress for women, and is generally worn with a head covering and perhaps a veil. Younger women might prefer a long cotton dress with a brightly patterned design.

In the past, high birth rates were partly kept in check by infant mortality. However, better health care has eradicated many of the endemic diseases. Since the 1960s, the government has been promoting family planning programs to keep the population at manageable levels. Such programs are still being pursued, but there is little sign of any success, except perhaps among the urban middle class.

LIFESTYLE

THE LIFESTYLE IN EGYPTIAN CITIES differs greatly from that of the village. Village people still tend to live in close communities that resist change. Everything here is dominated by the daily routine of tending the crops and livestock. The greatest change to the lifestyle of the rural people is the migration of an increasing number of young men to seek work in the cities.

City people, at least those that have acquired an education or wealth, often enjoy a far more cosmopolitan lifestyle. Clothing, entertainment and diet are often influenced by the Western world. However, Islamic beliefs and traditions form a common bond that unites Egyptians, and distinguishes the Egyptian lifestyle from that of other nations.

Opposite: **Life in rural Egypt moves at a leisurely pace. Here, a shopkeeper and his family take time off to pose for a picture.**

Left: **In contrast is this busy scene in Cairo, where life moves to a faster beat.**

In Egypt, children are thought of as a special gift, and people consider a large family to be a blessing from God.

CHILDREN

Egyptians love children and a big family is still considered a blessing from God. In the past, extra hands were needed to work in the fields, and children looked after parents in their old age. In a society where infant mortality was high, it was sensible to have as many children as possible to insure that some survived.

Young children are traditionally brought up in the kitchen by the women. The men of the family will make a great fuss over the children when they are together, but may not spend much time with them. As the children grow older the men may distance themselves further. This remoteness is sometimes felt necessary to retain the children's respect.

In the countryside, the child will usually be given the task of looking after the animals before going to school. After school there is homework, and then the boys will spend their time playing soccer, cards or watching television. Girls, however, are expected to help in the kitchen and so learn cooking and household skills. At harvest time, particularly in the cotton growing areas of the Delta, the children help work in the fields. Indeed, child labor is considered to be a serious problem and many children of poorer families work long hours to help the family income.

EGYPTIAN NAMES

Many Egyptian children are given names from the Koran. Mohammed is by far the most popular name for boys, but other religious names such as Ahmad, Khalid, Mostafa, Mahmoud, Omar and Osman are also very common. For girls, Fatimah and Eisha are examples of widely used religious names.

After the revolution, there was a spell when the old Arabic names returned to popularity. Children born during the 1960s and 1970s are more likely to have names such as Waleed, Wael or Walaa for boys, and Safa, Liala and Dalia for girls. The trend now, however, is to return to the Koranic names.

Circumcision was practiced as far back as the pharaonic times.

CIRCUMCISION

All male Moslems are circumcised, although this is not actually required by the Koran. In Egypt, circumcision is considered important for personal hygiene. Today, many baby boys are circumcised at birth. If not, the ceremony generally takes place before the boys are five, and certainly before they reach puberty.

In most cases, the operation now takes place at a doctor's surgery or health center. Circumcision is considered a very important event in a boy's life, and is a reason for feasting and celebrating. On the day of the circumcision it is customary for the boy to ride around the village on a horse. His family and friends will follow behind. Some of the men will carry guns which they will fire into the air.

Egyptian children attend primary school from the age of six to twelve. Those who are successful will go on to preparatory school.

EDUCATION

The Egyptian government provides free education, and primary school attendance is compulsory. After six years of primary school, some children will go on to three years of preparatory school, followed by another three years of secondary education. Secondary schools are divided into general schools and technical schools, which specialize in subjects such as agriculture and industry. Competition for the limited places in higher education becomes extremely fierce. At the top level, there are only five universities in Egypt as well as several institutes which run specialist courses in subjects such as drama, ballet or the cinema. In the past, it was the wish of every student to achieve a 90% pass rate in the university exam and gain entrance to the Faculty of Medicine. Although this remains the most prestigious career, some of the top students are now opting for other subjects.

Egypt has made enormous improvements to the education system since the revolution, and the illiteracy rate has fallen to around 66%, which is still high, but a great improvement on the figure of 50 years ago. It is estimated that up to 94% of children start school, but the drop-out rate is acknowledged to be very high. To encourage attendance, the new school year does not start until after the cotton harvest. At primary level, children will study mathematics, science, religion and Arabic. The government provides each child with a book for each subject, and in this way controls much of what is taught. The government also imposes regular exams on every child, and the tests which decide entrance to the next level of education are particularly important.

Despite all the effort the government has put into education, the system

A group of students congregates outside an examination center at Cairo's Al Azhar University, the oldest of Egypt's five universities.

is struggling under the pressure of the increasing population. It is not unusual to find 80 children in a classroom, or for a school to work morning and afternoon shifts. After teaching all day, many teachers then must do private tutoring to subsidize their low wages. Many middle class Egyptians are therefore opting to send their children to private schools. Before the revolution, there were over 300 private schools in Egypt, many of which taught in French. Today, a few fee-paying schools are reopening, often offering a combination of Arabic and English instruction.

A bride and bridegroom receive well-wishers at their wedding reception at a hotel. Most middle class Egyptian weddings are now quite Western-oriented, and the bride will often wear a modern white dress and stage a reception in the best hotel.

MARRIAGE

Marriage is a very important part of Egyptian life and is encouraged by the Islamic faith. Marriage is not only the joining of two people, but a union between two families who can support each other.

In the traditionally Moslem society there was little opportunity for young people to meet, so all marriages were arranged by the family. This is still the case in rural areas, where marriages are not only arranged within the village, but are often between cousins or other relations. Even in middle class homes, parents will probably make a great effort to introduce their teenage children to others their own age, who they feel will make "suitable" partners.

Many couples, particularly among the middle class, are no longer willing to start off married life with their parents. Apart from a home, a man could now be expected to provide furniture and a dowry. These responsibilities mean that it could take a man several years of working

Marriage

before he is sufficiently established to attract a bride. In the countryside there is little opportunity for newly married couples to have their own home, and the bride will start off life with her husband's family. She will be subordinate to both her husband and her mother-in-law, but her status will rise when she has children.

The wedding ceremony is very simple. In Egypt, marriage is a civil contract rather than a religious ceremony. All that is demanded is the signing of a formal contract between the bridegroom and the bride's male guardian, who is usually her father, but could be a brother or uncle. The contract must be signed in front of witnesses. In theory, any respectable Moslem man can act as witness. However, to make the marriage more "official," the wedding party will visit a special office to acquire the service of a government witness, called the Al Mazoun. The contract usually refers to a sum of money, *mahr*, which will become the wife's property in case of divorce.

After the service, it is important to announce the marriage, so there will be a procession from the house of the bride's family to her new home. Social custom demands that the wedding be followed by a great feast, with virtually all the people of the village invited. Even the poorest family will try to put on a show, even if it means going into debt to pay for it.

Moslem law allows a man to take four wives, but this is very unusual in Egypt and having only one wife is recommended and encouraged. Generally, a man will only take a second wife if his first has not borne children or becomes ill. Islam makes divorce easy, but the divorce rate in Egypt is very low, particularly in the rural areas where it would bring shame on both families. When a marriage has problems, all the relations will try to keep the couple together. The Koran also discourages divorce, and Mohammed described this as "the most hateful of all permitted things." If a woman is widowed, she will often be found a second husband within the same family.

A virtuous wife is a man's best treasure. The most perfect Moslems are those whose disposition is best; and the best of you are they who behave best with their wives. Paradise lies at the feet of mothers.

—A saying attributed to the Prophet Mohammed.

Egyptian women generally have more freedom than women of other Islamic countries in the Middle East. Although they may face powerful social pressures, there are few official restrictions.

THE ROLE OF WOMEN IN SOCIETY

Egyptian women enjoy more legal equality than women of many other Arabic countries. They are not compelled to wear veils or traditional Moslem clothing. They may vote, attend school, own property, drive cars and enjoy the same privileges as men. However, by Western standards, many women still seem to lead restricted lives. The emphasis placed on raising a family and looking after a home means that relatively few women reach influential positions. The government is trying to promote changes, and today many government companies have a deliberate policy of employing women in top management. Both the state-run television and radio stations have had women managing directors. Egypt has also sent several women ambassadors overseas.

However, although the government can lead the way, it is far harder to change the century-old attitudes of a whole country. In many families, the women's position in the home is as restricted as it has always been. It is virtually unheard of for a girl to leave the protection of her family until she is married, and after marriage she is expected to be submissive to her husband. Social customs generally do not permit single women to attend a dance or go to the cinema without the escort of a male family member. In rural areas, a woman might never leave her village except to go to market or attend a wedding.

Education is an area where there is supposed to be equal opportunity. However, in many schools, the boys are deliberately seated at the front of the class, where they receive more attention. Poorer families are certainly less likely to pay for a daughter to have extra tutoring than a son, or to allow a daughter to go on to higher education.

Although attitudes often restrict women, they also give them many rights and protections. Even in the most traditional home, Egyptian women still exert great authority. It is the women who will have control of money and legal papers, and who have a great say in the raising of the children.

Perhaps the most important change of all is the opportunity for Egyptian women to limit the size of their families. An increasing number of middle class women are releasing themselves from the endless toil and health risks of raising large families. It has been noted that even in rural areas many women are taking advantage of family planning advice.

There is concern that Egyptian women could lose many of the gains they have made if the mood of the nation changes. There are still members of parliament who campaign to make the veil compulsory, and a 1979 law allowing a woman to divorce a man who takes a second wife has come under heavy criticism as conflicting with Islamic beliefs.

In the countryside, women will tend to the household chores while their husbands work in the fields. Here, a group of village women wash their clothes and kitchen utensils in the Nile.

63

THE URBAN MIDDLE CLASS

Today, more Egyptians than ever are living in cities. Even for poor people, city life offers more job opportunities and the hope of a better lifestyle. For well-to-do city dwellers, Cairo or Alexandria offers a standard of living comparable with any city in Europe or America. City life, however, comes with its own problems. Traffic and pollution affect everybody. There are very few houses in Cairo, so even wealthy families are forced to live in an apartment. At least these apartments are large and comfortable. Although there is no garden, there is almost certainly a balcony where the family can sit outdoors. Children of middle class families are not likely to be allowed to play in the busy streets, and must try to amuse themselves inside their homes.

The apartment is likely to be filled with large and ornate furniture, and an enormous color television is usually the central feature. There may be lots of ornaments, but probably very few books. Few married Egyptian women will go to work, but will stay home to organize the house and meals. Times are changing, however, and younger girls in middle class families are very likely to be attending college or university.

Most middle class families will employ a maid who will live in the flat. She will look after the children and help with the housework. Sometimes another family will live on the roof, in homemade accommodations. They will be employed to keep the stairway tidy, and may do other small jobs for a little sum of money.

If the family plan a trip out, it will usually be shopping, or to visit relatives. Generally, Egyptians are not interested in concerts or museums. A surprising number of middle class Egyptians have never even been to see the ancient treasures in their national museum. After work and school, the family will often be content just to relax together with a meal and then watch television.

Egyptians can be extremely enterprising and sometimes it seems that everybody in Cairo has two or three jobs. Even Egyptians in good occupations often need to have extra sources of income to meet their expenses. An army doctor for example may run a private practice in the evenings. Perhaps he will also own an extra property in the city, which is being rented out. An accountant may do private bookkeeping in the evening, own a share in a relative's shop and occasionally drive a taxi.

Egypt has a serious urban housing shortage which the government is trying very hard to rectify. In overcrowded Cairo, many apartment buildings have been constructed to meet the housing needs of its growing population. Indeed, it is estimated that Cairo's population doubles every ten years because of the influx of immigrants from the rural areas.

SUPERSTITION

Superstition is deeply ingrained in the Egyptian culture. The most common fear is of "the evil eye," which is a spell that brings bad luck. This belief may well relate to the pharaonic story of Horus, who had an eye pulled out in his fight with Seth.

The evil eye can cause bad luck or sickness, but there are various ways to ward it off. God's name is often spoken out loud to give protection against bad luck, and people will mutter expressions such as *Bismillah* (In the name of God) or *Ma Sha Allah* (What God wills). Such expressions show submission to God and give him praise. These expressions can be worn in the form of charms and amulets. Other symbols worn to give protection include a blue bead, an open palm with the fingers spread out, or the pharaonic eye.

In the past, many babies died in Egypt, and the very young are therefore considered particularly vulnerable to evil spells. Charms, or even a dirty face, are thought to give some protection, as is dressing the child as a sheik or monk, or in cloth begged from others.

The evil eye is usually associated with envy, and it is therefore impolite to openly show admiration for possessions belonging to somebody else. In more rural areas, this would be considered quite suspicious behavior. If a person believes he or she is the victim of a spell, there are numerous things he or she can do to break it. An earth jar may be smashed behind the back of the person believed to be casting the spell. In the case of a spell that has caused illness, a paper doll should be pricked with a needle and then burnt. The ashes are then rotated over the sick person seven times before being thrown away.

The fellahin remain a very superstitious people, but even in the city you will still see everyday examples of superstitions. Good luck charms will dangle from the fenders of many motor vehicles. The charm often takes the form of an old shoe, and it is considered to be extremely bad luck if this talisman is ever lost. Many superstitions are now performed simply as habit. Tradesmen or shopkeepers, for example, will kiss and touch their forehead with the first piece of money they receive each day. This is a sign of thanks and praise to God.

Amulets, such as this eye of Horus, are worn to ward off evil spirits and to ensure safety and happiness.

FUNERALS

When a member of the family dies, the women of the household will start a ritual wailing. These cries and screams will carry the news of the death to the rest of the village. In all Moslem lands, the body is usually buried within 24 hours. This is a sensible practice in countries that are generally very hot. The corpse will be washed, dressed in a shroud and placed on a bier.

The body will then be lifted up and carried either to the mosque, or

directly to the cemetery. All the men of the family will takes turns at carrying the bier, and a long procession normally accumulates behind the body. It is generally considered a good deed to join a funeral procession, even if you have not known the deceased.

At the grave, an Imam ("EE-mahm") will lead the mourning and recite prayers to God and the Prophet. This will be followed by silent prayers and the actual burial. Moslems do not believe in cremation.

In the home of the deceased, the Koran will be read for several nights and food handed out to the poor. Richer families may decide to hold a wake on the evening of a burial. Brightly lit tents are erected for this purpose, and gilt saloon chairs hired for the guests to sit on. A wake may block a major road, but nobody is likely to show disrespect and complain.

The mourners are likely to be entertained by a *maqri*, a professional Koran reader. Some of the more famous professional readers enjoy a large popular following, and have become rich from their performances.

A wake can continue on successive Thursdays after the death, but any excessive show of grief can be frowned upon, as it is thought impious to protest against the will of God.

RELIGION

EGYPT HAS PASSED through three major religious stages. The ancient Egyptians had their own gods, such as Re, Horus and Anubis. One of the central themes of this ancient religion was a belief in the afterlife, and people went to incredible expense to provide tombs which would house and protect their bodies after death.

The religion of the ancient Egyptians proved remarkably resilient, and survived well into the Roman period. The Roman emperor, Theodosius I, did not order the old temples closed until the end of the 4th century A.D., and we must presume that the ancient gods continued to be worshiped in secret for some time after that. However, Christianity eventually swept away the old beliefs, and for three hundred years, Egypt became a Christian nation. This is referred to as the Coptic period. Even today, the Coptic Christians still make up the largest religious minority.

In A.D. 639, the country was conquered by the Arabs, who were driven by their own new and dynamic religion. The Arabic rulers did not force people to become Moslems, but there were considerable social and financial benefits for those who converted. As a result of this, Egypt today is predominantly an Islamic nation. Most Egyptians are Sunni Moslems who believe they have stayed the closest to original Moslem beliefs. Sunni Moslems are therefore often referred to as "orthodox" Moslems.

All Moslems believe in one god, whom they call Allah. Mohammed, who founded their religion, was his Prophet. Islam is seen as a complete way of life, combining creed and culture with manners and morals. By living according to Islam, Moslems believe that they will find peace with Allah, with each other, and with the world around them. Egypt does not practice such an extreme form of Islam as some of its neighbors in the region. For the past 150 years, Egypt has been moving away from being a strict Moslem state. Shari'ah courts, which give penalties according to the Koran, have been banned. Education is now run by the state rather than the mosques.

Above: **A devout Moslem, spreading his prayer rug, gets ready to pray, facing Mecca. Whether in the city, in the countryside or in the desert, when it comes to prayer-time, people will pray wherever they are.**

Opposite: **Constructed in the Turkish style, Mohammed Ali's Mosque is one of Cairo's outstanding landmarks.**

69

ANCIENT GODS

The ancient Egyptians worshiped many different gods or deities, who they believed could influence everyday life. The gods are either portrayed as human, animal or a combination of man and beast. Most gods were local to one town or district, but if that town prospered then the local god could gain wider popularity. Amon for example was originally the Sun God of Thebes. He came to be considered as the King of the gods and was later associated with the Sun God, Re, after which he was known as Amon-Re.

Central to the ancient Egyptian religion was a belief in the afterlife. Following an earthly death, a person was believed to go before Osiris and his 42 judges, who would weigh the dead person's heart against a feather. In the pyramids of the Old Kingdom, magic texts were carved on the walls to assist the king in his journeys in the afterworld. Such texts later found their way into the coffins of noblemen, and were collected together in the "Book of the Dead."

All the things people might need in the next world were placed in their tombs. For the pharaoh, this could include thrones, war chariots and whole chambers of golden objects. The dead person's body would be mummified, to preserve it for the afterlife. The organs would first be removed, and the body dried out. It would then be stuffed with resins and preserving oils, wrapped in strips of

Human and semi-human forms of some of the chief Egyptian deities.

ISIS
Queen of the gods and sister and wife of Osiris. Isis became increasingly popular during the New Kingdom.

RE
The Sun God, king of the gods and father of mankind. Portrayed as a man with falcon's head and sun disk. Holds an ankh and scepter.

ANUBIS
The embalmer and god of the dead. Shown as a black jackal or a man with a jackal's head.

HATHOR
Goddess of love, birth and death. Shown as a female goddess with horns or ears of a cow.

SETH
Started as the god of the oasis but lost popularity, possibly due to his role in the legend of Osiris.

THOTH
Moon God, inventor of writing and god of learning. Depicted with an ibis' head.

linen, and placed in the tomb.

Ancient Egypt underwent drastic religious changes during the reign of Amenhotep IV. He tried to sweep away the old gods and convert the country to a new religion. Amenhotep IV worshiped the God Aton, who was represented by the disk of the sun, and he even changed his name to Akhenaton. A new capital, called Akhetaton (Tell el-Armarna), was founded in a remote area between Luxor and Cairo. This move may well have been an attempt to get away from the influence of the powerful priests of Thebes. Certainly religious conflict appears to have been the main cause behind the civil unrest in the country at this time. After the death of Akhenaton, people quickly returned to worshiping the old gods, and the priesthood became more powerful than ever. However, we do not understand everything that went on in ancient Egypt. It was always presumed that the new capital was quickly abandoned. Latest excavations, however, suggest this was not the case. The new city continued to be occupied, and even expanded in the years immediately after Akhenaton's death.

Although Akhenaton's religion did not last, it is still considered to be a very important event. It was the first religion in the world that believed in only one God, and it is possible that Moses may have been influenced by stories of Aton. If so, then Akhenaton's strange new religion would have helped mold Judaism, and from there influenced Christianity and Islam.

NEPHTHYS
Goddess of women and sister of Isis.

HORUS
Originally a god of Lower Egypt but became the god of the ruling pharaoh. Associated with the falcon. Son of Isis and Osiris.

OSIRIS
God of agriculture and of the afterlife. Murdered by his brother Seth, and resurrected by Isis.

PTAH
In Memphis, Ptah was believed to be the creator of the world. He was the patron of craftsmen.

SOBEK
Protector of reptiles and god of water. Shown as a man with crocodile's head.

AMON
King of the gods and patron of the pharaohs. Often identified with the Sun God Re, as Amon-Re.

EGYPT: AN ISLAMIC NATION

Islam is the second most widely practiced religion in the world today. Followers of Islam are known as Moslems, and they believe in one God, called Allah, who is the creator of the universe and judge of mankind. Mohammed is the Prophet of Allah.

THE KORAN

The Koran, (also spelt Qur'an), is the sacred scripture of Islam, and Moslems believe the book contains the words of Allah, as told to his Prophet, Mohammed. Many Egyptians have a Koran in their homes, probably displayed on a decorated stand. A Koran must never be put on the floor. In many cases, this may be the only book in the house. The Koran is divided into 114 chapters, known as *Surahs*, each with its own name. The chapters can vary in length from a few lines to several hundred verses. It is written in half prose and half poetry, and contains language of great power and beauty, especially when read out loud. The first chapter, *al-Fatiha*, is recited by devout Moslems every day as part of their prayers.

The Koran is regarded by Moslems as the final and complete revelation of God, so care is taken never to make the slightest alteration in any way. Because of this the Koran cannot officially be translated. Of course, translations do exist, but they are considered to be only for study purposes, and should not be used for worship.

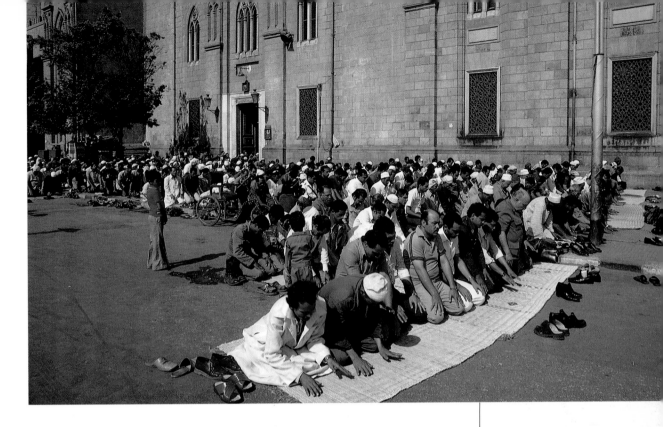

PRAYING FIVE TIMES A DAY

Prayer is very important to Moslems and they are expected to pray five times a day. When praying, they should kneel and face towards Mecca. By praying, they remind themselves of the central belief of their religion, "There is no God but Allah, Mohammed is the Prophet of Allah." It is obviously not always practical to go to the mosque five times a day and people will pray wherever they are. A farmer in the field will kneel by his crops, a man in his office might simply leave his desk for a few moments. Moslems are, however, encouraged to pray together, and many Egyptians will at least try to attend mosque for the second prayer on Friday.

The call to prayer is given by the muezzin. Traditionally, he was a blind man. Not only would this give him employment, but he would not be able to look down from the minaret into people's courtyards. In modern Egypt, the muezzin may well have a loudspeaker to help him. The call to prayer will also be given over the television and radio.

If women attend the mosque, they will pray separately from the men. It is far more common for women to pray at home, particularly in the villages where they are kept busy with their household duties.

Facing Mecca, Moslem faithfuls prostrate themselves during prayer-time. Prayers are done five times a day: between first light and sunrise, after midday, in the late afternoon, after sunset and after dark.

73

Above: **Islamic studies being conducted at Al Azhar Mosque. Founded in A.D. 972 by the Fatimid dynasty, Al Azhar has been a place of prayer and a training center for missionaries, religious judges and teachers for centuries.**

Opposite: **Wall paintings depict the experiences of those who have made the pilgrimage to Mecca.**

THE IMAM

Islam emphasizes the closeness between human beings and God, and any Moslem man of good faith can lead the prayers. A woman may also lead the prayer, but only if there are no men in the congregation. However, most mosques do appoint a trained Imam. Apart from reading the prayers, he might teach lessons in the Koran and answer people's questions regarding the interpretation of Islamic laws. The Imam will also be expected to give a sermon on Friday after the prayers. This gives the Imam considerable influence over his community. The government approves the major religious appointments, and also controls who is permitted to give sermons on television and radio. However, Imams who build up reputations as dynamic and controversial speakers can draw thousands of people to their mosques. Popular sermons are sold on tape cassettes, and in this way reach an even bigger audience.

THE HAJJ

It is the duty of every Moslem to visit the holy city of Mecca at least once in their lives, unless prevented from doing so by reason of poverty or illness. Every year, thousands of Egyptians will make the hajj, and when they return to their villages many pilgrims will paint murals on the outside of their houses, showing scenes from their journeys. Apart from religious rituals, many of these murals will often include pictures of aircraft or passenger ferries. This is a good reminder that for many Egyptians the hajj may be the only chance they will ever get to see the world outside.

The hajj is performed during the second week of the 12th month of the Islamic calendar. At the start of the hajj, the male pilgrims will put on a *ihram,* which is made from two white sheets of seamless cloth. This symbolizes purity and makes all people equal, whatever their status or wealth. There is no prescribed dress for women, but they must go unveiled.

The pilgrims now enter the "haram," the sacred area around Mecca which is forbidden to non-Moslems. At the Great Mosque, they will walk seven times around the Ka'bah. The Ka'bah is a 40-foot long and 50-foot high block of black granite and is the central shrine of Islam that all Moslems face when praying. Moslems believe the Ka'bah marks the place where heavenly bliss and power touch the earth directly.

The pilgrims now perform the sa'y (sah-ee), a ritual which involves running between the hills of Safa and Marwah seven times. Then the hajj moves on to Mina, some five miles east, where the night is spent in prayer and meditation. Starting when the sun passes the meridian, the pilgrims will stand and pray on the plain of Arafat. This is where Mohammed preached his last sermon. The afternoon of prayer and meditation is considered the supreme experience of the hajj and will continue until just before sunset.

The night is spent at Muzdalifah and the pilgrims then return to Mina just before daybreak. They spend three nights here. On each day, they throw seven stones at each of three pillars. Casting the stones symbolizes the casting out of evil. At the end of the hajj, they sacrifice an animal as a gesture of renunciation and thanksgiving, and the meat is given to the poor.

A Coptic priest conducts a service. On his right hand is the Cross of Saint Mark, patron saint of the Coptic religion.

THE COPTS

The Coptic Christians are the largest religious minority within Egypt. They are particularly numerous in Middle Egypt, around the city of Asyut. There are also large Coptic communities in Luxor, Cairo and Alexandria. An official government survey estimated there were just over two million Christians in Egypt, although the church claims the figure is really around five million. The Coptic community is indistinguishable from the Moslems in language, dress or physical appearance.

The Christian religion started to gain strength in Egypt around A.D. 300. It was believed that Christianity was brought to Egypt by Saint Mark. At first the Christians were persecuted by the Romans, and many sought refuge on the edge of the desert. First, they lived as hermits, and then formed small religious communities. This monastic life is still an important part of the Coptic religion today, and there are several large and active monasteries in Egypt.

Christianity prospered in Egypt after it became the religion of the Roman empire, and the Greek Church of Alexander was soon ruling over forty bishoprics in northern Egypt. In A.D. 451, the Alexander Church broke away from the Church of Rome over the issue of "Monophysitism." The Egyptian church retained the belief that Jesus had a single and godly nature.

The church of Rome took the belief that Jesus had both a human and a godly nature. This difference still separates the Egyptian Coptic Church from other main branches of the Christian faith.

Today, the Coptic religion is led by its own pope. The present pope is Shenouda III. Sunday is the Copts' main religious day. This is a working day in Egypt, but Copts are permitted time off from work to attend church. Churches normally run two services, the first between seven and nine in the morning so that people will not be too late arriving at their offices. Hymns are an important part of the service, and might be sung in Arabic, or the old Coptic language. If sung in Coptic, only a very few people will actually understand the words they are singing.

Outnumbered by the Moslems, the Copts tend to maintain close communities, and in the past established their own schools. Today, these schools are open to anybody and might have many Moslem pupils. The present government has a policy of tolerance toward the Copts, and there have been some prominent Christians in high office.

A Coptic church—the focal point of Copts' identity. Coptic services still use a language that is a variation of that spoken in ancient Egypt.

SAINT MARK

Saint Mark, the most important saint of the Coptic people, was one of the leading figures in early Christian history. He accompanied Saint Paul on his first missionary journey, and later journeyed to Crete with Barnabas. According to tradition, he was the author of the second Gospel and the founder of the church in Alexandria. He is believed to have died a martyr's death.

LANGUAGE

Opposite: **Shop signs display both the Arabic and English language. Besides Arabic, most educated Egyptians are fluent in English or French, or both.**

ARABIC is the national language of Egypt. It originated in the Arabian Peninsula and is classified as a Semitic language. This places it in the same group of languages as Hebrew and Ethiopic. Nobody knows for sure when Arabic developed, but with the Arabic military success it spread throughout the Middle East and North Africa.

Today, it is one of the major languages in the world. It is the official language of 17 countries and is spoken by more than 120 million people. It is also the language of the Koran, and so has religious significance to millions of people who are not native speakers.

DIFFERENT TYPES OF ARABIC

Arabic appears in different forms. There is classical written Arabic, which is the language of the Koran. Although described as a written language, it may be spoken in sermons or used in plays. Novels written in a more modern form of Arabic may also use classical Arabic to record the conversations.

There is spoken, colloquial Arabic, which differs from region to region. There are nine major dialects, and a person from Lebanon or Iraq might struggle to understand an Egyptian. Indeed, northern Egyptian and southern Egyptian make up two of the major dialects. Generally, all Egyptians can understand each other. However, two Egyptians meeting for the first time would certainly be able to distinguish whether their new acquaintance came from Cairo or Upper Egypt, by the way they spoke. The nine major dialects of Arabic differ from classical Arabic and from each other, in vocabulary, grammar, pronunciation and syntax.

Above: **The *al-Ahram*, the best known of three daily newspapers in Egypt, is read by a wide segment of the public. In addition, there are two daily French-language newspapers, and one in English.**

79

Because of the regional differences, Egypt has been developing a third language, sometimes called "modern literary Arabic." This is the written language of newspapers, documents, and works of non-fiction. It is simpler than classical Arabic in grammar, syntax and vocabulary. Because it avoids the local dialects, it is understood throughout the Arabic world. Therefore, although it started out as a written language, the spoken form is becoming increasingly used for speeches, television and radio.

As it has always used the Koran as a guide, modern literary Arabic has stayed quite close to classical Arabic. Arabic people would probably have considerably less trouble reading an ancient classical manuscript, than English-speaking people would have understanding a novel written in medieval English.

WRITING IT DOWN

Arabic writing uses 28 symbols and is read from right to left or from top to bottom of a page. Many of the letters are flowing and circular and look very attractive. There has been a long tradition of competitions to copy out sections of the Koran, so handwriting has become a respected art form. Indeed the word "calligraphy" comes from Arabic and means "the art of handwriting."

There are many different scripts. Originally the Kufic script that developed in the Iraq city of Kufah was the most widely used. However, Naskhi, a rather plain script, gained popularity. Today, this is the main script used because it is very clear and ideal for modern printing. Other scripts are used for different purposes. Official documents might be written in Diwani or Diwani Jali. Both are very ornate and formal looking scripts that were brought to Egypt by the Ottomans.

Arabic calligraphy with the words, "In the name of Allah, the Compassionate, the Merciful." Arabic calligraphic script has its origin in the days when it was used to embellish the Koran.

Egyptian greetings are often punctuated with colorful expressions and questions.

WONDERFUL EXPRESSIONS

Arabic is a colorful and exciting language, containing many wonderful expressions. Many of these have a religious meaning.

"Insha Allah," for example, means "If God wills it," and is spoken after every prediction: "Tomorrow, I will go to Luxor, insha Allah," or "My car will be ready tomorrow, insha Allah."

"Al Hamdulillah" ("al HAHM-du-lee-lah") means "praise be to God," and is often placed at the end of a sentence: "We have a wonderful house, al Hamdulillah," or "Our plane arrived safely in Cairo, al Hamdulillah."

"Maalehsh" ("MAH-lesh") means "it doesn't matter," or "too bad," or "don't take it seriously," and is another common expression. A man who has just smashed his car into a wall will climb out and mutter "maalehsh." This is partly to save face, but is also an acknowledgment that things could be worse.

Greetings are often prolonged with a whole series of colorful expressions and questions. A man may wish somebody he meets a good morning. In return, he may be wished, "morning of light." The first man may then reply with "morning of Jasmine." Most likely, this introduction would be followed by a series of questions inquiring about the person's health and family. In each case, whatever the truth, it is customary to answer that everything is wonderful—always with "al Hamdulillah" at the end of each statement.

SPEAKING WITH THE REST OF THE WORLD

Arabic does not translate particularly well into other languages. Because it uses a different alphabet, there are often disagreements about how things should be spelled. Asyut, for example, can also be spelled Assiut. The soccer player, El Khatib, can find his name written Al Khatib, and Fayyoum and Fayyum are the same place.

In today's modern world, learning a foreign language is becoming increasingly important for young Egyptians. Traditionally, rich Egyptians would learn French, but today English is considered the most important language to learn.

Above: **Egyptian students are encouraged to learn languages besides Arabic.**

Opposite: **The streets of Egypt's cities offer a wide variety of reading material.**

ARABIC WORDS IN ENGLISH

During the early spread of Islam, the Arabic people were a dynamic force. Apart from being a great military power, they led the world in trade, science and navigation. Just as today we see English giving the whole world a computer vocabulary, so 800 years ago Arabic lent many words to other languages.

From Arabic astronomers we have adopted the names of many stars, such as Altair, Algol and Aldebran.

From their traders we borrowed the names satin, cotton, sequins, tariff, checks, saffron and caraway.

Their mathematicians gave us the words algebra and average.

While their chemists gave the world alcohol and alkali.

Right: Egyptian hierogly-phics incised in stone. The written language of the Egyptians, it con-sisted of 750 signs. Most are pictures of people, animals, plants or ob-jects.

Below: The hieroglyphic alphabet. Some of these signs had the value of one letter of our alphabet, but others represented two or more.

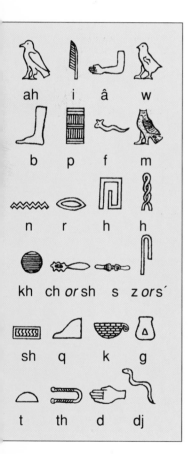

ah	i	â	w
b	p	f	m
n	r	h	h
kh	ch or sh	s	z or s´
sh	q	k	g
t	th	d	dj

THE LANGUAGE OF THE ANCIENT EGYPTIANS

The hieroglyphic language first developed around 3000 B.C., with symbols or drawings to represent objects and actions. The name hieroglyphic was given by the Greeks, and means "sacred carvings." In the earliest times, only the priests used hieroglyphics, and they were known as "the speech of the gods." Slowly, some pictures became simplified, and others came to stand for a sound rather than a concept. Eventually more than 3,000 word signs and pictograms existed, but many were only used very occasionally.

The size of the vocabulary made it a very difficult language to master and as time went on, it was only used for carvings in monuments and temples. During the Middle Kingdom, a style of writing known as Hieratic came into everyday use, and by 400 B.C., a newer, demotic script had evolved. Hieroglyphics, however, remained in use for religious services until A.D. 400, but eventually died out during the Roman rule.

The scribes who kept records belonged to a very honored profession,

THE ANCIENT EGYPTIAN PUZZLE

At the start of the last century, much of ancient Egypt remained a mystery to us. There was a whole world of information carved onto tomb walls, or written on papyrus, but this was in an old and forgotten language that could not be translated.

All of our written information came from the early Greek travelers, whose notes and books we could read. However, there was only a tiny amount of such information, and it had been written long after the Egyptian civilization had gone into decline.

Then, in 1799, there was a wonderful discovery. An officer in Napoleon's army found a slab of black stone outside the town of Rosetta. The stone had three types of writing carved into it—the first two were the ancient Egyptian hieroglyphics and demotic languages. The third, however, was Greek—a language that was still understood.

For the first time, scholars had a key to unlock the written treasures of ancient Egypt. However, the task was not easy; imagine having one page of a book in English and a copy of the same page in French—and from that being asked to teach yourself French.

The man credited with breaking this ancient code is Jean François Champollion. He was a genius, who at 11 had taught himself most of the European languages and who at 18 was a professor of history at Grenoble University. The Rosetta stone became his great challenge. By comparing the Greek with the Egyptian text, he could work out some of the meanings and sounds of the ancient language. He also understood Coptic, a language related to that spoken by the ancient Egyptians, and this knowledge enabled him to decipher other words.

However, it was not until 1822 that Champollion translated the whole text and published his findings. At last, the lost world of the ancient Egyptians was unlocked and open for us to explore.

The Rosetta Stone was an incredibly fortunate find, and nothing similar has been discovered since. Today, the Rosetta Stone is one of the many Egyptian treasures in foreign museums and people wishing to see it will have to visit the British Museum in London, although there is a copy in Cairo.

and people who could afford to do so sent their sons to school to learn the written language. The students spent hours copying out examples of hieroglyphics. Writing was done on "papyrus," which was the world's first paper-like material. It was made from a tall reed that grew in the Nile. Pens were made from reeds, with softened and sharpened ends, and ink was manufactured from a mixture of soot and water.

ARTS

EGYPT HAS A LONG ARTISTIC TRADITION, and poetry, music and the decorative arts are an important part of Egyptian culture. These remain extremely popular today.

However, over the last 150 years, Egypt has come under great influence from the Western world. Today, Egyptian painters, film producers and novelists are combining these Western art forms with ideas and feelings from their own experiences and culture.

LITERATURE

Egypt's literary heritage dates back to pharaonic times. At first, writing in ancient Egypt was only for administrative purposes, but by the 4th and 5th dynasties we see the first biographies appearing in the tombs of important noblemen. It was the Middle Kingdom that produced the classic period of ancient literature. By this time the culture was rich with stories, songs and myths. There was also a great deal of instructional material on subjects such as magic, medicine, astronomy and mathematics.

Egyptian writers made good use of puns, similes and metaphors. The appearance of the work on the paper was also very important. Ancient Egyptian script was normally written from right to left, but could also be arranged left to right, or top to bottom to create a more pleasing effect. Songs and poems were probably the most popular form of literature, perhaps because they were easy to read aloud in a land where very few people could understand the complex hieroglyphics. Much of the poetry was religious, and some was similar in style to the psalms in the Bible. The Egyptians wrote little fiction, except for some simple stories of travel and adventure.

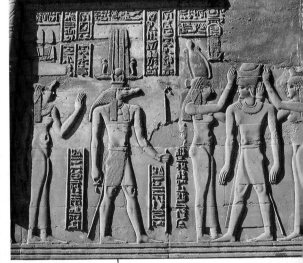

Opposite and below: **Modern mural art at an alabaster factory in Luxor takes its inspiration from the hieroglyphics of ancient Egypt, which, besides being functional, were used for their decorative effect.**

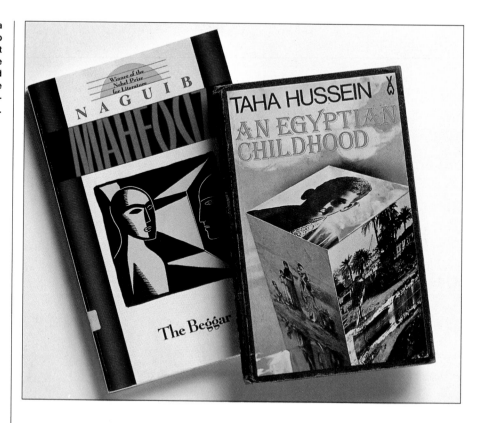

Writers such as Taha Hussein and Naguib Mahfouz have brought Egyptian literature to the world's attention and many of their works have been translated or published in other languages.

There were no plays at all, although some of the well known myths were no doubt acted out.

Under the Arabic influence, folktales and *makama*—a narrative essay—became popular. It was poetry, however, that was the most important style of writing. Many of the poems were aimed at ordinary people, and were memorized and recited.

Poetry is still extremely popular in Egypt today, although modern Egyptian literature is shaped by many different influences. More people read magazines than books in Egypt, and so the short story has become a good way for writers to reach a wider audience. Since the revolution, more Egyptian writers have turned their attention to full length novels. However, the novel is really a Western concept, and it has taken time for Egypt's authors to develop their own style. Some of the earliest novels looked at Western influence on Egypt. Tawig al Hakim's *The Bird from the East* and Yahya Haggi's *The Camp of Umm Hashim* are good examples of this subject.

NAGUIB MAHFOUZ—NOBEL PRIZE WINNER

Egyptian writing came to world attention in 1988 when Naguib Mahfouz was awarded the Nobel Prize for Literature. Born in 1912, Mahfouz was the son of a minor government official. When he was growing up there were no Egyptian novels, so he had to seek his first inspiration from the work of European writers such as Tolstoy and Proust. He studied philosophy at the university and then entered the university administration.

His first novels were set in pharaonic times, but he was to become famous for his stories of the bazaars and alleyways of Cairo. *Midaq Alley* is his most famous book. He has also written a remarkable trilogy named after the streets and squares of Old Cairo. In *Palace of Longing, Between Two Palaces* and *The Sugar Alley* he traces the life of a merchant family from the years 1919 to 1944. In doing so, he creates a wonderful set of characters and captures the atmosphere of the old city in much the same way that Dickens once described Victorian London. However, he also uses the books to examine the hopes and disappointments of the Nationalist Movement.

Such works have secured Mahfouz's place as the leading writer of the Arabic world.

Mohammed Husayan Haykal's book, *Zaynab,* was one of the first important books to look at life in the Egyptian countryside, although the author took a rather romantic view of his subject. A more realistic style was pioneered by Taha Hussein. Hussein was born in a small village in Upper Egypt and he lost his sight when he was three years old. His auto-biographical novel, *An Egyptian Childhood*, and his numerous essays have brought him considerable fame. Like many successful writers, he was rewarded with high positions in government service. He was also nominated for the Nobel Prize for Literature.

Many Egyptian writers need financial help to continue their work. There is a limited market for their books at home, and Arabic does not translate easily into other languages. Those that do not win government support might turn to writing plays or film scripts, or write only as a hobby. However, following the international success of Egypt's greatest writer, Naguib Mahfouz, more Egyptian novelists may find their work being translated and sold abroad.

FILM

Cairo is known as "The Hollywood of Arabia," and Egypt produces a thousand or more movies a year for distribution throughout the Middle East. The first films were being made in Egypt before World War I, but it was the founding of Misr Studios in 1934 that really marks the start of the Egyptian film industry.

The man who first brought Egyptian films to a world audience was Yusaf Shahin. In 1940, he directed and starred in *Babal-Hadid*, the story of a Cairo street urchin. For this movie, as in most of his work, Shahin avoided using big stars, but instead selected and trained ordinary people from the street. The other great Egyptian director was Shadi Salam. He was born in Alexandria and attended the faculty of Fine Arts. Salam learned his film craft by assisting some of the best Egyptian directors of the day, and was soon acknowledged as an expert on historical costume design.

Throughout his career, Salam was happiest working on films that featured Egypt's ancient past. His titles include *The Golden Chair of Tutankhamun* and *Ramses II*. Shadi Salam was so highly respected that when he died in 1986, the then prime minister was sent to represent the government at his funeral.

These days, low budget films or soap operas with an emotional storyline, often involving sentimental romances, are popular as they help people escape the humdrum of their own lives.

Watching movies is a popular form of entertainment in Egypt. In Cairo, the cinemas, which show both Arabic and subtitled foreign language films, are usually full. An Egyptian star who gained an international reputation is Michel Shalhoubi, better known by his adopted name of Omar Sharif.

THEATER

The only traditional form of Egyptian theater is a shadow play performed by puppets. Made from either paper or leather, the puppets are operated with sticks or strings, and their shadows are cast up onto a white screen. These one-act plays were performed at least 700 years ago, and are still shown in Cairo today. Shows normally take the form of a one-act play and are very funny, with comical characters and lots of jokes. The puppets are often a lot ruder in their actions than human actors would be permitted to be.

Although simple "folk plays" have always been performed in the villages, modern drama was imported into Egypt from other parts of the world. Professional theater in the Middle East started in Syria during the last century. The political persecution of the Turkish authorities forced many troupes to flee to the safety of Cairo. Salim Khalil al-Naqqash was one of these political refugees, and in 1878 he wrote *The Tyrant*, the first play ever performed in Arabic. Around the same time Ya'qub ibn Sanu made a major contribution to Cairo theater with his comedies and operettas. He was the first of the early play writers to use the local spoken dialect rather than classical Arabic.

The best known of all the modern play writers was Taufiq al-Hakim. As a young man he was sent to Paris to study law, but spent much of his time involved in theater and musical performances. He returned home to build a reputation of being one of Egypt's most exciting and original writers. He wrote plays such as *The Bargain,* which paid tribute to the Egyptian fellahin. Although he usually wrote in classical Arabic, Hakim would often use folk dances and songs to make his work familiar to the people.

Cairo is the cultural center of the Arab world. Cairo's opera house and its many theaters entertain thousands each year with many excellent productions.

91

MUSIC AND DANCE

Music and dance was important to the ancient Egyptians. They composed beautiful songs and hymns which were highly praised by the early Greek travelers who heard them. Music was seldom played on its own, but used to accompany singers. At first, the leading instruments were harps and the six-hole flute. By the New Kingdom, the Egyptians had either invented or imported lutes and clappers.

A musician in Luxor plays a traditional stringed instrument. Songs, music and dance are as much a part of Egypt today as they were centuries ago.

The Arabic invaders had their own instruments, some of which were already known to the Egyptians. The lute became the most important instrument but the viola, tambourine, drum and rabab (a fiddle) were also used. The Arabic people paid little attention to sports or fine arts, so music became the main art form.

The music of this period should really be divided into classical Arabic and folk. The classical music was used in the mosques for religious ceremonies and remained strict and formal. Folk music was simpler, and subject to change. A farmer in the fields or a boatman on the Nile might equally sing an age-old chant, or repeat the classical music he had heard at the mosque.

Today, both classical Arabic music and folk music is coming under pressure from European influences. No village anywhere in Egypt is likely to be without its transistor radios, and the sound of big stars such as Madonna would be recognized by most Egyptians. Indeed, the best of the modern Egyptian music is often considered to be that which combines European influences with Egypt's traditional sounds. Sayed Darwich has earned the title "father of modern Egyptian music" with his compositions that blend classic Arabic music with European opera. In a lighter vein, Mohammed Abd El Wahab, has done a similar job of creating songs which combine the style of European pop with elements of Egyptian folk music.

The most famous Egyptian singer of all was the female vocalist Umm Kulthum. Her music was very Egyptian sounding, sung at a slow pace, with a backing of traditional instruments. Some of her songs might last an hour or more, and at the end it was not unusual for the crowd to demand a repeat performance of the same number. When she died, the streets of Cairo were jammed with people following her funeral procession.

Keeping in touch with tradition. Dancers at a local hotel perform a folk dance.

Egyptian folk dancing is closely linked with traditional Egyptian music. Folk dances were originally developed to celebrate different stages of the agricultural cycle, and would also be performed at weddings or festivals. The dances vary from region to region, with the most distinctive dances coming from the far south and from the oasis regions.

Egypt is also famous for the belly dancing of its women. The belly dance originates in Turkey, but is much admired by many Egyptians. There are several versions of the dance, some of which use candles, both held in the hand and fastened to a headdress. The light from the candles emphasizes the skill and grace of the dancer's movements.

One unusual legacy of Russian influence is the Cairo Ballet Company which was founded in 1960 and trained by the famous Bolshoi Ballet. The first ballet written in Egypt was *The Difficult Day*, a dance inspired by the 1967 war.

A carpet designer puts his pen to paper. Cottage industries flourish in Egypt, where craftsmen, using traditional skills handed down through the generations, transform raw materials into works of art.

ART

The Arabic people have little tradition for fine arts, and such work has still to make much impact on Egyptian culture. However, there is an Egyptian School of Fine Arts, and the government encourages art work with exhibitions and competitions. Mahmoud Mokhtar is the best known of the modern Egyptian artists, and many of his imaginative sculptures are now displayed in his own museum in Cairo. Another artist, Haji Ahmed Uthmar has become equally famous for his work with Islamic decorative arts.

Some exciting tapestry work also takes place at the Wisa Wassef school of weaving. Ramses Wisa Wassef founded the school by teaching weaving to the people of Harraniyyah village. At the time, this community was quite isolated, and the ideas and inspiration for each tapestry came from the weaver's own village environment. As a result, animals and country scenes feature in nearly all the tapestries. Any one piece of work might take months to complete, and the colors and style often reflect the changing mood of the artist. The second generation of weavers are now practicing their craft, and the work is highly prized. Kings and millionaires have visited the workshops, and Wisa Wassef tapestries hang in some of the greatest museums in the world.

FOLK ART

Although lacking in fine art, Egypt has a wealth of folk art. For centuries, care has been taken to make everyday objects decorative. This is partly to make them pleasing to the eye, but also to enable them to serve as an investment. The traditional materials used are brass, copper, ivory, silver and gold. Wood is seldom used, simply because Egypt does not have any forests. The same materials are still used today, and much of the work is carried out in the same way as it has been for centuries.

Brilliantly colored, a woven rug conveys scenes of rural life.

Copper and brass ware of all shapes and sizes hang from a shop in Cairo. Many of these items are still worked by hand using traditional methods.

COPPER AND BRASS Although the sheets of metal are now produced in factories, copper and brass objects are still hammered out by hand in small family workshops. Mirror frames, trays, plates, vases, coffee pots and smoking pipes are the most common objects to be manufactured. However, new ideas that will please the tourists, such as name plates and Christmas tree ornaments, are also being produced.

When damp, copper becomes toxic, so any item intended to be used in cooking should be lined with tin or silver. To make the metal more durable and easy to work with, it is often mixed with other metals. Brass, which is a common working metal, is a combination of copper and zinc. It has a golden color which makes it popular for decorative pieces.

To make the items more attractive, they might be embossed, chased or inlaid.

JEWELRY Many Egyptians from the countryside have little knowledge or faith in banking and prefer to invest in gold or silver. This is kept in the form of jewelry, and has created a whole industry to design and manufacture decorative items. The villagers favor large and bulky items, and this style still influences even modern designs. Earrings, necklaces and bracelets are the most common pieces. Other influence has come from Arab calligraphy and the tourists' demand for pharaonic reproductions.

Left: **A craftsman polishes raw inlaid boxes, before transforming them into exquisite finished products, in a Cairo bazaar.**

Below: **Bangles, bracelets and earrings dangle from a silver shop in Cairo.**

INLAID WORK Many boxes, chests or chessboards are decorated with tiny pieces of mother-of-pearl, inlaid into the wood to form mosaic patterns. Ivory was also once used for such work, but is now too expensive for most craftsmen.

MASHRABEYYA Mashrabeyya is the name for Egypt's beautiful wooden latticework windows. Because they were cool, but still offered privacy, they became extremely popular in the 19th century, despite the fact that the wood to make them had to be imported. Most of the old mashrabeyya windows have been taken to museums, but some shops still practice this old craft. Carpenters, today, are assisted by a few modern electrical tools.

LEISURE

RELAXING sometimes seems to be the most popular pastime in Egypt. The hot desert climate and a life of hard labor in the fields have made people value any time that is left free just to sit and talk with friends. In the villages, the women will gather together in the courtyard of a private house to chat and exchange stories. Most men, however, are likely to spend at least some evenings in a coffee house.

THE COFFEE HOUSE

A typical Egyptian coffee house is often a large, tiled saloon, possibly with sawdust on the floor. Waiters with trays will squeeze between the tables, and shoeshine boys will hover, hoping to catch the eye of a customer. The saloon is usually noisy with the bubbling of coffee brewing, the clack of dominoes, the slap of cards being thrown on the table and the crackle of rolling dice. Discussion and arguments are a vital part of the entertainment, and there will be a cheerful exchange of views between the patrons. Indeed, the art of conversation is well developed in Egypt, and people are res-

pected for their wit and humor. Lively conversations on politics or local events are embroidered with a wealth of proverbs and religious quotations. In the countryside, where fewer people are literate, one man might read out articles from the day's paper to an interested group of listeners.

Many coffee houses cater to a particular group of people. Some attract homeless fellahin, others intellectuals, while another may be favored by retired army officers.

THE EGYPTIAN WATER PIPE

Whether you call it a nargileh, a hubble-bubble pipe, or simply a water pipe, the traditional smoking instrument of Egypt is an important part of the atmosphere of any coffee house. A water pipe stands on the ground, by the side of the table, and has a glass or brass base filled with water. The tobacco is burnt over live coals, and the smoker uses a three-foot long, snake-like tube, to draw the smoke up. As the smoke passes through the water, it is filtered and the taste lightened. The action produces a gurgling sound which many people find soothing.

Regulars to a particular coffee house might keep their own personal pipe there. Many men also enjoy smoking a water pipe at home, and it is often the job of the children to have this ready when father comes in from work. Women very seldom smoke a water pipe, and would certainly not be expected to do so in public.

Ma'assil is the favorite tobacco and is a sticky blend of chopped leaves fermented with molasses. There are dozens of brands of *ma'assil* that are sold nationwide, and hundreds of local brands particular to one town or province.

Alternatively, smokers might prefer *tumbak,* which is loose dry leaves wrapped into a cone.

After some years of declining popularity, the water pipe is once again becoming fashionable. The rising price of cigarettes partly explains this, but many rich people are turning to the water pipe in an effort to rediscover their own culture. However, it shouldn't be forgotten that the water pipe, like any form of smoking, carries serious health hazards.

GETTING OUT OF DOORS

Families in the cities are far more likely to spend leisure time together. In Cairo, people will often arrange an evening's picnic. The city has few parks or gardens, but the banks of the Nile have grass areas which make a pleasant place to sit. However, on a warm evening, people will converge on any open spot, and even the grass center of a large highway will be crowded with families enjoying being out in the open air.

Many wealthy people now own a villa at Alexandria where they can escape the Cairo crowds. It is also becoming fashionable for Egyptians to explore their own country. On national holidays, the desert around the pyramids is crowded with people enjoying a day out. The beaches of Alexandria and the Bitter Lakes are other popular day trips from the capital.

The lively, airy seaside city of Alexandria with its wonderful beaches is a popular spot for those who love the sun and the sea.

RECREATION IN ANCIENT EGYPT

It was probably only the wealthy people in ancient Egypt who enjoyed much leisure time. In those days, as is often the case now, the farmers would have been kept busy just growing sufficient food to feed their families.

The affluent, however, had many ways of enjoying themselves. We know that sailing in small papyrus boats on the Nile was popular. While on the river, people might try to harpoon fish, or hurl throwing sticks at the ducks and geese which nested in the reeds.

More serious hunting also took place, and the ostrich, gazelle or oryx might be pursued with the help of hunting dogs. Hunting was a sport and was good training for warfare. We even have pictures of men harpooning hippopotamuses, which must have been an extremely dangerous activity.

The Egyptians played several board games, including one which was a type of chess, and another that was similar to backgammon. They also had dice, although we are not sure what games they played with them.

Music was very popular. Some of their instruments were quite easy to make, so it seems likely that even the poor people were able to enjoy playing tunes on a simple flute.

We know that the pharaohs were entertained by dancers and nimble girl gymnasts. It seems likely that there would have been traveling troupes who made a living from entertaining in the villages. Similarly, storytellers and poets probably toured the land—some telling their tales at the royal court, others entertaining in the poor neighborhoods.

There seems to have been no organized sport in ancient Egypt. However, people practiced juggling with balls, and this was often incorporated into the acrobatics' performances. A tomb at Tell-el-Amana also shows two figures playing a game that looks very much like modern field hockey. Wrestling was popular, but there is no record of any competitions being staged.

THE INFLUENCE OF TELEVISION

The increasing popularity of television is making major changes to the way families spend their spare time. Popular soap operas or important soccer matches might persuade the whole family to stay in for the evening. Many villages are also acquiring TV sets, and it is not unusual to see a room crammed with children, all watching an American-made cartoon. Even the traditional atmosphere of the coffee house is being challenged, and an increasing number now have a television set placed in one corner.

A NATION OF SPORTS LOVERS

Egyptians love sports, and the country has adopted all the major international games. Most schools will usually have at least a small courtyard, which will be used for marching, parades, and sporting activities such as basketball and volleyball. Boys may also get a chance to play some organized sport when they complete their national service, while some of the bigger firms run teams for their staff.

The first sports Egypt excelled at were wrestling and weight lifting. At the 1928 Olympics, weight lifter Nasser El Sayed broke the world record, and won Egypt's first ever Olympic title. At the 1936 Berlin Olympics Egypt did even better, winning three medals.

The men's Olympic swim squad is probably the best in Africa, and long distance events are particularly popular. Egypt's best swimmers have successfully completed all of the great marathon events around the world. Rowing and sailing are other popular water sports. Yachting takes place at al-Maadi, just a few miles south of central Cairo, or on the open sea at Alexandria.

Although north African runners are now ranked among the best in the world, Egyptian track stars have not yet reached such high standards. However, Egyptian throwers are the best in Africa.

Squash is another event that has seen Egyptian sportsmen win world class tournaments. By African and Middle East standards, Egypt can put out strong teams in hockey, tennis, volleyball, handball, water polo and basketball. Apart from winning many regional events, Egypt has played a leading role in developing sport in Africa and the Middle East. Egypt regularly plays host to regional championships. The biggest event to be staged in Egypt so far has been the 1991 African Games. This is an Olympic-like event that brings together teams from all over Africa.

Cyclists outfitted in their professional gear get all ready to go. Cycling is another popular outdoor activity in the city.

Despite the hot weather, women will be expected to keep their legs covered when playing activities such as tennis. Even on the beach, girls who have reached puberty will often go swimming in a full tracksuit.

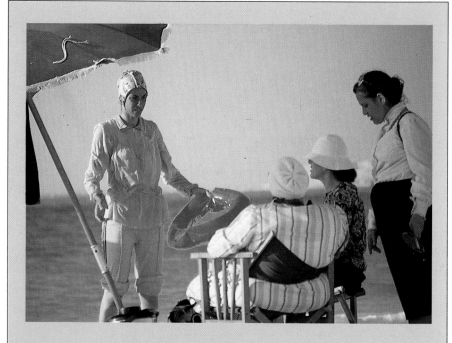

WOMEN AND SPORTS

Egypt sends a large team to the Olympic Games, but the majority of their competitors are always men. In the last two Olympics Games, Egypt has not sent one woman to compete in the track and field events. Similarly, although the men's team traditionally do well in the African volleyball and basketball championships, the women's team is never represented in the finals.

In middle class families, it is now becoming acceptable for young women to play sports such as tennis and squash. Younger girls might enthusiastically practice gymnastics and swimming. Some of the big sports clubs stage "women's only" afternoons in the gymnasium or pool, where sportswear can be worn without conflicting with local dress codes.

However, although women are slowly being encouraged to take part in recreational exercise, it is certainly not considered normal for them to take sports seriously. Those who wish to must fight against serious social pressure such as chauvinistic attitudes which are still strong in Egypt, modesty and dress codes which create problems and prevent women from competing at a serious level, and societal pressure to marry young and start a family. Serious training for sport would in most cases be seen as conflicting with these "more important duties."

EL AHLY

ZAMALEK

ARAB CONTRACTORS

The club colors are very important to Egyptians fans, who will often go to matches wearing the same shirts as their favorite teams. Banners and flags add to the colorful spectacle, and it is often more fun to watch the spectators than the game.

SOCCER: THE GREAT LOVE

Soccer is the undisputed king of Egyptian sport. When a big match is being played at the national stadium, the streets of Cairo are deserted, with everybody who is not at the stadium, staying home to watch the game on television. If Egypt scores an important victory, the whole nation will celebrate. Processions of cars will drive around the streets with flag-waving supporters sitting on the roofs. However, when a favorite team loses, fans can often run wild, breaking windows and damaging buildings close to the stadium. The players take the game equally seriously and tempers often flare up on the pitch.

Soccer was brought to Egypt by the British, but the local people soon learned the game and by 1907 had formed their own club, El Ahly. The Egyptian Football Association was founded in 1921 to help develop the sport. Egypt played in three Olympic tournaments between 1920 and 1928 and scored victories over Turkey, Portugal and Hungary. They also played in the 1934 World Cup but lost their only game.

During the 1950s, Egypt helped to organize the sport in Africa, and the African Football Confederation is still based in Cairo. It was an Egyptian army officer, General Abdelaziz Mustapha, who donated a trophy for African national teams. Egypt has won this trophy three times, most recently in 1986. Besides that victory, Egypt's other great success was in reaching the 1990 World Cup finals. They played three games against top teams such as Holland and England, and only lost one match.

At home, the favorite club is El Ahly, who nearly always win the Egyptian league. However, they are usually given a tough fight by their great rival, Zamalek. Many Egyptian teams are owned or sponsored by big firms, such as Mehella, which is sponsored by a giant textile firm, and Arab Contractors, which is heavily supported by the Osman building company.

FESTIVALS

THERE ARE TWO MAIN TYPES of holidays in Egypt, religious holidays and those which celebrate important dates in recent Egyptian history. In addition, the Coptic community celebrates their own religious dates. Most of the Islamic holidays are based on the Higra calendar, and as a result occur a little earlier each year, compared with the modern Gregorian calendar.

Festivals are generally not so important to Moslems as to people of other religions. Partly this is because Islam attempts to discourage any connections with pagan traditions, and partly it is because Islam is a religion that should be practiced every day. Even the two official holidays of Eid al-Adha ("ihd ahl-AHD-ha") and Eid al-Fitr are not mentioned in the Koran.

However, over the years, peoples' love of special festivals has led to other holidays being added to the calendar. The Prophet's birthday is the best example, and is an important holiday in Egypt. However, it was not celebrated for the first time until at least 400 years after Mohammed's death.

All Moslem holidays are usually celebrated with extra prayers, sermons, lavish meals, and visits to relatives.

Above: **On religious festivals like Eid al-Fitr, which celebrates the end of the fasting month, children are dressed in their best.**

Opposite: **A sheep is slaughtered for a feast. On Eid al-Adha, which marks the end of the holy pilgrimage, even the poorest family will slaughter a lamb or sheep to eat.**

RAMADAN

Observing the holy month of Ramadan is one of the five pillars of the Moslem faith, and Egyptians take Ramadan very seriously. Moslems are expected to fast during Ramadan, and they should not eat or drink while the sun is up.

To decide when the fast is over the Imam in the mosque holds up a white and a black piece of thread. When he can no longer tell the difference between the colors, it is considered night, and the fast is over.

On Eid al-Fitr, Moslem families gather together to celebrate the end of Ramadan. Those who are working away from home will try to return for this festive occasion.

The streets then become empty as everybody eats. Many people will stay up late to have supper before sleeping, and then will get up just before daybreak to have a last meal before the fast begins. The long day without refreshment is usually very hard on everybody, and Egypt's hot climate makes it particularly difficult to go without drinking.

People often become very tired during the month, and the whole pattern of life changes. Government offices will slow down or even stop work altogether, and it is not unusual to go into an office and find everybody sleeping at their desks. Schools will often close early so that students can go home for an afternoon nap.

Not everyone has to fast. Young children are excused, although many might fast for a day or two. The sick and old are also excused. Travelers, soldiers on duty and women who are menstruating need not fast. However, this group of people should try to make up the fasting days at a later time.

People will be more diligent about their prayers during Ramadan and many families will put time aside to read the Koran. Indeed, most families aim to read the whole Koran by the end of the month. Each evening, there is usually a large gathering outside the mosque as the people celebrate the end of another day of fasting. These crowds build up in numbers and excitement as the end of Ramadan approaches.

EID AL-FITR

Eid al-Fitr is the most important holiday in Egypt and it celebrates the end of the month of Ramadan. It is the one day that everybody should be with their family, and in the days leading up to Eid al-Fitr the airports and harbors will be crammed with overseas workers returning home for the holiday.

Ramadan is also a time to be aware of the plight of the poor. Each year, at the end of Ramadan, all Moslems should pay *zakat,* by giving a certain amount of their wealth to the poor. This is not a charity because Moslems are not really given any choice about giving. Neither is it a tax. *Zakat* is instead considered to be an act of worship. Indeed, the name means "purify" and it reminds everybody that all wealth really belongs to Allah.

EID AL-ADHA

Also known by the Turkish name of Qurban Bairam, this holiday marks the end of the holy pilgrimage. The main feature of the celebration is the lavish feasts. In the days leading up to the festival, everybody who can afford to do so, will buy a sheep or goat. These will be left in the street outside the house to impress the neighbors and flaunt the family's wealth. On the 70th day after Eid al-Fitr the animals will be slaughtered for the feast. One third of the sacrifice will be given to the poor.

Youths in a festive mood celebrate a holiday.

MUHARRAM

Muharram is the Moslem New Year, and marks the day Mohammed and his followers set out for Mecca on their flight from Medina. The day is not celebrated as much as New Year's Day is in the Western world, but families are likely to get together and exchange gifts. The Islamic calendar is based on the phases of the moon, and so only has 354 days. This means that the major festivals occur 12 days earlier each year, compared with the calendar used in the United States and Europe. Egypt also seems to come to a stop on the Western new year, with many people missing work and families going out together.

SAINTS' DAYS

In the past, local Saints' days, called Mulids, were reason for villages to stage elaborate celebrations. Events might include fairgrounds with bright lights and blaring music, acrobatics, belly dancing and camel racing. There would be a religious feast at the local mosque.

Saints' days celebrations are now more subdued, or in many cases have died out altogether. The police objected to them as they often led to riots and crime. The Islamic authorities supported the suppression of Saints' days as such events were unorthodox and thought to have pagan links. The only Saints' day to be widely celebrated is Mouled al-Nabi ("MOO-led ahl-NAH-bee"), the birthday of Mohammed himself. This is an important national holiday on which it is traditional to give children gifts of sugar dolls and sweet pastries.

COPTIC HOLIDAYS

Coptic celebrations usually fall later than in Europe. Christmas, for example, is celebrated on January 7. The religious holidays are celebrated with church services and family gatherings. The Coptic people pay particular attention to the Saints, and on special Saints' days large numbers of people will make the trip to once remote monasteries.

A large extended Coptic family gathers together to celebrate the occasion of a baptism.

SHAM EL-NESSIM: A LEGACY FROM ANCIENT EGYPT

The ancient Egyptians had numerous local festivals such as the "Festival of the Living Falcon" and the "Festival of the Victory of Horus." One of the most important events was the "Festival of the Sacred Wedding," when the statue of Hathor was taken from the temple of Dendera and rowed a hundred miles south to Idfu. It would arrive to coincide with the rising of a new moon. On that night, the statue of Hathor would be reunited with that of Horus, Hathor's legendary husband.

The most important holiday, however, was the Spring Festival, which celebrated the reawakening of the earth after winter. In ancient times, this holiday also marked the start of the Egyptian year, which would then run through the agricultural cycle. During the Spring Festival, people would eat eggs, which were seen as a symbol of renewal after death. The idea of eating eggs as a special celebration was adopted by the Jewish religion, and then copied by the Christians. It continues in the Christian world today with the giving of chocolate Easter eggs.

The statue of Horus.

The ancient Spring Festival has survived the centuries, and today is known as Sham el-Nessim. This translates from the Arabic as "breathing of the spring air." Its celebration occurs at the time of the Coptic Easter, and it is a holiday that is particularly important to the Christian people. However, it is a national holiday, and is celebrated by both Christians and Moslems. Sham el-Nessim probably bears little resemblance to celebrations that took place in ancient Egypt, but the eating of eggs has remained a tradition. Ordinary hens' eggs are used, but they are boiled in a coloring to dye them brown. Salted fish and onions are also traditionally eaten on this day and are thought to prevent disease. Many families will rise very early to go for a picnic by the Nile or in the countryside.

NATIONAL HOLIDAYS

The anniversaries of historical events that have occurred since the revolution give the Egyptians several other national holidays. There are no real traditions associated with such days, although many families take the opportunity to get together for a meal. The anniversaries will however be commemorated by special reports and articles in the newspapers and on television. There will also be some formal or social event organized by schools and factories. Armed Forces Day was always celebrated by a large military parade, and it was at such an event that President Sadat was assassinated. Since then, there has been no central parade, although the different governorates may stage some military show. National Day, on July 23, celebrates the 1952 Revolution and is the most important of the non-religious holidays.

MAIN HOLIDAYS

MOSLEM

Moslem name	Meaning
Muharram	New Year's Day
Mouled al-Nabi	Birthday of Prophet Mohammed
Eid al-Fitr	Celebrates the end of Ramadan
Eid al-Adha	Marks the end of the pilgrimage

COPTIC

Christmas	January 7
Epiphany	January 19
Easter	varies
Annunciation	March 21
Feast of Virgin Mary	August 15

NATIONAL HOLIDAYS

New Year's Day	January 1
Sinai Liberation Day	April 25
Evacuation Day	June 18
National Day	July 23
Armed Forces Day	October 6

OTHER HOLIDAYS

Sham el-Nessim

FOOD

Opposite: **A bountiful harvest of carrots—produce of the Nile. Fresh salads and vegetables are served with most meals.**

Below: **An Egyptian meal, comprising among other things, unleavened bread, *foul* bean dish and a meatball dish.**

EATING IN EGYPT often turns into a social event. Whether it is a family gathering, or a group of men meeting for business, a meal may stretch out over numerous courses and finish with several cups of coffee. Sometimes the food may even seem to take second place to the conversation.

TYPICAL MEALS

Egyptians will often have five meals a day, although some of these will be light snacks. The typical breakfast, at least in the city, is usually just a drink at home, and some *foul* ("fool") beans and bread bought from a stall on the way to work. By mid-morning, most people will have taken a light meal of bread, coffee or tea, and perhaps some combination of cold meats, pickles or eggs.

Lunch will most likely be eaten in the afternoon, and for a poor family consists of just bread and cheese and a few vegetables. People in towns will probably have something more elaborate, such as rice, salad and some type of meat. Egyptians, in fact, eat a great deal of rice, and yellow saffron rice topped with boiled lamb is a typical dish. Rice is also used to make a sweet dessert.

An evening meal is served when the family arrives home. This probably consists of cooked meats, and vegetables with rice. There will be bread again, and perhaps olives and salads. Poorer families, however, may just serve some kind of stew with bread.

A late supper at around ten o'clock will finish off the day. A typical supper will consist of a *foul* bean dish, perhaps with another favorite such as fried vegetable balls, or grape leaves stuffed with rice.

For those living in the cities, a variety of reasonably priced cafes or restaurants is available.

Although Egyptians like sweet foods, they are not noted for their desserts. Often, they will finish a meal with fruit, particularly red watermelon. However, one noticeable exception is bassboussa. This is a cake made from yogurt, semolina, milk and butter, which is baked golden brown and covered with syrup.

Meals cooked in even the richest Cairo homes will be similar in ingredients to those eaten in the poor rural areas. City people, however, will generally eat more, and have a greater variety in their diet.

Even today the fellahin in the villages have a diet that is not particularly healthy or well balanced. Bread and corn or millet make up the bulk of the food, along with some vegetables. There may be a little cheese, dates and melons but fish and meat will only be served on special occasions.

Biram Ruzz

Bassboussa

THE VOCABULARY OF EGYPTIAN FOOD

Baba Ghannooj A cold dip made from eggplant, lemon and spices.

Bassboussa A sweet semolina cake served with syrup poured over it.

Biram Ruzz A creamy rice and chicken casserole.

Burghul Cereal made from whole grains of wheat.

Felafel Deep fried balls of chickpeas and crushed wheat.

Foul Beans, usually cooked for several hours and then served in bread. Sometimes crushed to form a dip, as with *foul midammis.*

Hummus Chickpeas pureed into a seasoned dip.

Mansaf A special Bedouin feast of lamb and rice.

Milookhiyya An edible green leaf that resembles spinach. Often used to make soup.

Tahina A thick paste made from crushed sesame seeds.

Sacks full of dried herbs, cumin, saffron, ginger, coriander and all manner of spices can be found in the spice markets of Egypt.

EGYPTIAN SPECIALTIES

Several vegetables play a bigger part in Egyptian cooking than they do in Western countries. Eggplant is perhaps the best example. These purple vegetables, also known as aubergine, were first brought from India over 1,500 years ago and have found their way into numerous recipes. They may be used in a dip such as *baba ghannooj* or baked with grilled lamb or mutton in a moussaka.

Okra, the green pods from the plant of the same name, is also widely used in Egyptian cooking. It often forms the base of a stew or soup.

Olives are also great favorites in Egypt, and they were one of the first fruits to be cultivated by man. Egyptians seldom use olives for cooking, but serve them as a snack with bread and cheese. The most common Egyptian cheese is feta, a soft white cheese made from sheep's or goat's milk.

Egypt is on the traditional spice route between Asia and Europe and a good Egyptian cook will make use of a variety of spices such as cumin, caraway seeds, saffron, camphor and myrrh. There are whole markets in the town that sell nothing but spices.

FOOD IN ANCIENT EGYPT

Thanks to the fertile waters of the Nile, the ancient Egyptians enjoyed a variety and abundance of food that would have been the envy of the other early civilizations. There was always the danger of the floods failing and bringing famine, but in good years Egypt must have seemed a land of plenty.

Many of the foods they ate were surprisingly similar to meals still enjoyed by the people living along the Nile today. Then, as now, bread was probably the staple food and the ancient Egyptians were among the first people to learn the art of making leavened bread. They had many different recipes for bread, including some in which the dough would be flavored with dates, fruits or spices.

The ancient Egyptians also discovered the art of brewing, and beer was made from barley, wheat or dates and spiced bread. Beer was drunk with most meals, perhaps because ordinary water was considered unsafe.

We know that Egyptian gardens grew a wide variety of produce including asparagus, cabbages, celery, onions and grapes. Lentils were widely used in soups and stews. Cattle, ox and sheep were kept for meat and milk, while poultry and fish were important parts of the diet.

Cooking was done in mud ovens, in roast pits or over open fires. At the table, people used clay dishes, and the wealthy would have special metal drinking cups. There were spoons and knives, but much of the food would have been eaten with the fingers.

The selection and preparation of food was very important, and food offerings were often made for the dead. Indeed, much of our information about diet in ancient Egypt comes from drawings in tombs. There are pictures of great feasts where a whole oxen would be roasted. However, we have far less information on the food eaten by the poor people

OTHER INFLUENCES

For several hundred years, Egypt was part of the Ottoman Empire, and their cuisine still reflects this Turkish influence. For example, dishes such as kebab and moussaka are basically the same as you would find in other countries around the east Mediterranean.

In recent times, Egyptian food has also come under international influence, and it is possible to find expensive restaurants serving European food, or cheap hamburger bars. The middle class Egyptians might eat in a foreign restaurant on a special occasion, but most Egyptians generally prefer their own food.

RELIGIOUS INFLUENCE

Religion has had a major influence on Egyptian eating habits, and pork is only eaten by the Christians. Meat must be slaughtered in the proper manner. This means cutting the windpipe and carotid arteries of the animal while the *bismillah* is quoted from the Koran. This is an acknowledgment that God is the creator of all things. The meat is then "halal" or permitted.

Alcohol is also forbidden under Moslem laws and no Moslem should drink alcohol or sell it to a non-Moslem. However, there is a large brewing industry in Egypt and beer can be bought in most restaurants. Beer will often be provided for guests at weddings and other family feasts. During Ramadan, people will be far stricter, and during the holy month restaurants and hotels usually only sell alcoholic drinks to foreigners.

MEAT

With people being forbidden to eat pork, and the land not being suitable for beef cattle, sheep and goat provide most of the meat. Camel meat, however, is popular in the poorer homes and pigeons also play an important part in Egyptian cuisine. Many houses in the countryside keep an elaborate dovecote, and roasted pigeon is a delicacy that is often offered as the main course of a feast.

Seafood was traditionally supplied from the Mediterranean coast. However, modern methods of transportation have allowed the Red Sea to be developed as an important source of seafood.

Flanked by the Mediterranean Sea and the Red Sea, Egypt has abundant seafood.

Egyptians have a sweet tooth and they like a lot of sugary cakes and pastries.

A SWEET TOOTH

In most towns you will find special cake shops selling Egypt's popular sweet pastries. These are called "halva" and "baklava."

Baklava are small sweet pastries made from layers of paper-thin dough. Halva are similar, but are made from semolina or rice flour. These sweets go by delightful names such as "lady's wrist" and "eat and promise."

There are many different types of halva and baklava, and they differ mostly in their fillings. Some are filled with dried fruits such as dates, figs and apricots. Others are decorated with chopped nuts such as pistachios or walnuts. To make them especially sweet the baklava are dipped in syrup, or, for better quality, honey.

Surprisingly, these pastries are not usually eaten after a meal, but are ordered with tea or coffee as a snack. The biggest shops will display trays of 20 or more different types of sweets, and whole teams of bakers will work non-stop replenishing the stocks. Each flavor is distinguished by its shape.

DRINKS

In Egypt's hot dry climate, drinking is very important. Teas spiced with mint, jasmine, rose or saffron are popular and were originally drunk as mild medicines and tonics. Tea in Egypt is often made from cheap tea dust, so people will normally drink it with lots of sugar. Hibiscus leaves are also used to make a drink called *karkadeh*.

Although tea is becoming increasingly popular, it is coffee which should really be considered the Egyptian national drink. Coffee might be served at the end of a meal, presented to guests who arrive during the day, or be drunk in cafes where men gather to talk and relax after work.

Egypt's cafes serve drinks from Turkish or Arabic coffee to teas spiced with mint, jasmine or rose. And there's nothing like having a friendly game of dominoes and a smoke in convivial surroundings.

There are two similar, but different ways of serving coffee in Egypt. One is Arabic coffee, the other Turkish. Both are served black in small cups, and both are made from green beans that have been roasted brown and then pulverized with a mortar and pestle or a coffee mill.

Turkish coffee, however, is made in a coffee pot which narrows from the bottom to the top. This shape intensifies the foaming action as the coffee boils. Water, sugar and coffee are stirred in, to meet the customer's individual taste, and the pot is whisked off the fire as soon as it boils. It is returned to the fire at least once more to build up a foaming head. When the whole process is done, the coffee is poured into the cup along with the coffee grounds, which settle to the bottom of the cup.

Arabic coffee is different because it is prepared in a single boil and sugar is seldom added. Once it boils, the coffee is poured into a second pot, leaving the sediment behind. Arabic coffee will probably be flavored with spices such as cloves or cardamom seeds.

STREET FOOD

Virtually every street corner in Egypt has a stall selling food. Each day millions of people in the big cities will stop on the street to purchase a quick and filling snack.

Such stalls are particularly busy at breakfast time. The most popular breakfast is a spoonful of *foul* beans, flavored with oil and lemon juice, and placed inside a round, flat, bread that has been split open. A chopped salad is added as garnish. Because beans and bread are cheap, such a meal only costs the equivalent of a few cents. In Egypt, beans are known as "poor man's meat." However, *foul* for breakfast is equally popular with rich Egyptians.

Felafel is another favorite street food. It is ground chickpeas, mixed with *burghul* and spices, and then deep fried. These can be eaten as they are, or placed inside a pita bread with some kind of sauce.

Other vendors may specialize in fried eggplant, stuffed peppers, baked sweet potatoes or simply sell slices of coconut. In the villages, or neighborhoods in Cairo, the vendors usually operate late into the night, and the stalls will be lit by bright kerosene lamps. Some stall owners may even provide a few simple chairs for their customers.

Kebab is another popular meal that people buy on the street. However, this requires more equipment and is usually sold from the front of small shops. Marinated lamb slices are pushed onto skewers that are slowly rotated over a gas or charcoal fire. The outside cooks first, and when there is a customer the chef will cut paper-thin slices from the outside of the meat, dropping the pieces into a split round of bread.

Wayside stalls selling food and drinks are found all over the streets of Egypt. Operating from morning to night, they are patronized by Egyptians from all walks of life.

BREAD

Bread forms the central part of the Egyptian diet, and people will eat it at virtually every meal. Egyptian bread is round, hollow, flat and about the size of a small dinner plate. The bread can be split down the middle, and food placed inside, rather like putting a letter into an envelope.

Even a big dinner will still be served with a plate full of bread, and it has been estimated that many Egyptians eat as much as three pounds of bread each a day.

Bread consumption is so high that Egypt now has to import wheat. Because it is such an important part of the diet, the government subsidizes the cost of bread, and a few cents will buy you an armful. The cost of this subsidy is a heavy burden on the country, and one the government would like to either see reduced or removed.

However, bread is a major political issue. In 1977, when the government did attempt to increase bread prices, there were food riots in Cairo. Since then the government has allowed only token increases to the price of bread.

A man on his rounds delivering bread. Each year, the Egyptian government spends over a billion dollars to provide the people with cheap bread.

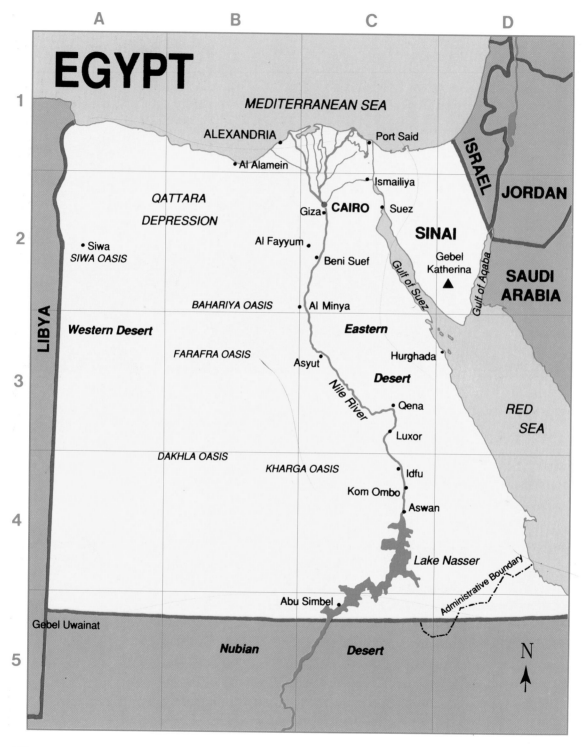

EGYPT

MEDITERRANEAN SEA

ALEXANDRIA
Port Said

• Al Alamein

ISRAEL

JORDAN

Ismailiya

QATTARA
DEPRESSION

Giza • **CAIRO** • Suez

SINAI

• Siwa
SIWA OASIS

Al Fayyum •

Gebel
Katherina
▲

SAUDI
ARABIA

• Beni Suef

BAHARIYA OASIS

• Al Minya

Eastern

Western Desert

FARAFRA OASIS

Asyut •

Desert

Hurghada
•

RED
SEA

• Qena

Nile River

Luxor •

DAKHLA OASIS

KHARGA OASIS

• Idfu

Kom Ombo •

Aswan •

Lake Nasser

Administrative Boundary

Abu Simbel •

Gebel Uwainat

Nubian

Desert

N
↑

LIBYA

Gulf of Suez

Gulf of Aqaba

124

Abu Simbel   C5
Al Alamein   B1
Al Fayyum   C2
Al Minya   C2
Alexandria   B1
Aswan   C4
Asyut   C3

Bahariya Oasis   B2
Beni Suef   C2

Cairo   C2

Dakhla Oasis   B4

Eastern Desert   C3

Farafra Oasis   B3

Gebel Katherina   D2
Gebel Uwainat   A5
Giza   C2
Gulf of Aqaba   D2
Gulf of Suez   C2

Hurghada   C3

Idfu   C4
Ismailiya   C2

Kharga Oasis   C4
Kom Ombo   C4

Lake Nasser   C4
Luxor   C3

Nile River   C3
Nubian Desert   B5

Port Said   C1

Qena   C3
Qattara Depression   B2

Red Sea   D3

Sinai   D2
Siwa   A2
Siwa Oasis   A2
Suez   C2

Western Desert   A3

—— International Boundary
▲ Mountain
● Capital
● City
✕ River
◗ Lake

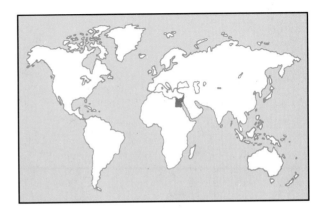

QUICK NOTES

OFFICIAL NAME
Arab Republic of Egypt

LANGUAGE
Arabic

RELIGION
90% Sunni Moslems, large Coptic minority

RULING PARTY
National Democratic Party

LAND AREA
386,650 square miles

MAIN GEOGRAPHICAL FEATURES
Nile Valley and Delta, Western Desert, Eastern Desert, Sinai Peninsula, Lake Nasser (artificial), Suez Canal (artificial)

POPULATION
56 million (1990 estimate)

CAPITAL
Cairo

CURRENCY
Egyptian Pound
(US$1=3.27 Egyptian pounds)

CHIEF PRODUCE
Oil, cotton

MAJOR POLITICAL LEADERS
Mohammed Naguib—First president of the Arab Republic of Egypt (1953).

Gamal Nasser—Leading member of the revolution which overthrew the monarchy, he replaced Mohammed Naguib as president in 1954. He introduced sweeping reforms such as land reforms and nationalization of banks and the cotton industry.

Anwar Sadat—Became the president when Nasser died of a sudden heart attack in 1970. The first Arabic leader to visit Israel, he was assassinated by Moslem fundamentalists at a military parade in 1981.

Hosni Said Mubarak—As president, oversaw Egypt rejoining the Arabic world. In the 1990 Gulf Crisis, he ordered Egyptian troops to join U.N. forces to free Kuwait.

GLOSSARY

delta   Fan-shaped area of land that forms at the mouth of a river.

demotic   A cursive form of Egyptian hieroglyphics for everyday use.

fellahin   Egyptian farmers.

felucca   A long, narrow vessel, propelled by oars or lateen sails, or both.

Imam   A religious leader or a prayer leader of a mosque

irrigation   A system of canals, pipes or ditches that provides water for farming.

khedive   A Turkish governor of Egypt from 1867 to 1914.

oasis   A fertile spot in the desert watered by a spring, stream or well.

papyrus   A water reed, common in ancient Egypt, used for making paper, and also light boats.

BIBLIOGRAPHY

Kay, S.: *The Egyptians: How They Live and Work,* David and Charles, Vancouver, 1975.

Feinstein, S.: *Egypt in Pictures*, Lerner Publications, Minneapolis, 1988.

Macaulay, D.: *Pyramid,* Houghton Mifflin, Boston, 1975.

Odijk, P.: *The Egyptians*, MacMillan, New York, 1989

Worthington, Dr. E.B.: *The Nile,* Wayland/Silver Burdett, NJ, 1985.

INDEX